WINNING RECIPES
from our
Members and Leaders

OVER 60 RECIPES LOW IN POINTS

Edited by Sue Ashworth

SIMON & SCHUSTER
A VIACOM COMPANY

First published in Great Britain by Simon & Schuster UK Ltd, 2001.
A Viacom Company.

Simon & Schuster UK Ltd.
Africa House
64–78 Kingsway
London WC2B 6AH

Photography: Steve Lee
Styling: Marian Price
Food preparation: Wendy Lee
Design: Jane Humphrey
Typesetting: Stylize Digital Artwork
Printed in China

Weight Watchers Publications Manager: Elizabeth Egan
Weight Watchers Publications Executive: Corrina Griffin
Weight Watchers Publications Assistant: Celia Whiston

A CIP catalogue record for this book is available
from the British Library.

ISBN 0 743 40918 3

Pictured on the front cover: Sticky Pork, (page 35); Better Brownies (page 56);
Spicy Turkey Marrow (page 29); Red Cherry and Ginger Slice (page 47).
Pictured on the back cover: Chocolate Mousse (page 44).

V denotes a vegetarian recipe and where relevant assumes that vegetarian cheese and
free-range eggs are used.

contents

WINNING RECIPES

Welcome to WINNING RECIPES from our
Members and Leaders...

First of all, thank you to everyone who entered our Members and
Leaders recipe competition. We had thousands of fantastic recipes
sent to us which made the judging very difficult but it was also
very enjoyable!

Congratulations to all the contributors to this book; we
were delighted by the high standard of delicious low point recipes
which you sent in and the result is a unique cookbook, which we
are all proud of. We have no doubt that it will inspire thousands
of Weight Watchers Members to cook and eat tasty food while
still losing weight.

Special congratulations must go to our Category Winners:
Jane Ferguson, Elena Graham, Shuba Singhal, Eileen Walling,
Judith Warrington and Alison Winter and our Low Point Winners:
Sue Coats, Valerie Gough, Hazel Ross, Megan Thomas, Rachel Wells
and Anne Wilkinson.

From the judges: Sue Ashworth; Celia Whiston and Corrina Griffin.

We hope that you will enjoy the recipes we have chosen and we are sure that there is something for everyone here. In *Winning Recipes*, you will find over 60 delicious recipes which include low point versions of your traditional favourites such as One Pot Chicken (page 37) and Roly Pavlova (page 51) as well as ingenious creations to tempt the tastebuds such as Gammon in Raisin Sauce (page 41) or Rhubarb Lasagne (page 52) which are definitely worth a try. There are dishes to suit all the family and all budgets and they don't need too much preparation – they can fit easily into today's hectic lifestyles.

As you know, with the wonderful pure points™ no foods are forbidden – if you fancy it, you can eat it! Simply make sure that you count the points and stay within your daily allowance. Within pure points™ there is so much room for interesting, innovative recipes and you will see that the dishes which have been developed for this book reflect the enthusiasm and dedication of our Members and Leaders. This delightful array of low-fat, low-calorie recipes is inspiring for us all because they have been developed to provide maximum flavour with minimum points by fellow dieters – perfect!

One thing that we have discovered is that so many of you use our All Day Snack Bars and Chocolate Crisp Bars to create scrumptious desserts or snacks. Similar ideas came in from lots of you and we thought that this would be a great opportunity to share the best ones with everyone. Thanks to all of you who sent the following – we think they are fantastic:

BARBECUED CHOCOLATE BANANAS

POINTS	per serving: 3

(V) *Serves 1*
Preparation and cooking time: 20 minutes (barbecue) or 15 minutes (oven)
Calories per serving: 155

Slice a Weight Watchers Chocolate Crisp into 5 pieces and layer alternately with the slices of 1 medium banana. Wrap in tinfoil and barbecue for 15 minutes or put in the oven at Gas Mark 5/190°C/ 375°F for 10 minutes or until the banana is cooked and the chocolate has melted. Delicious on its own but if you have the extra Points to spare, serve with a (60 g) scoop of low-fat ice cream. Each scoop is 1 Point.

CHOCOLATE ORANGE 'BOWL'

POINTS	per serving: 3¹/₂

(V) *Serves 1*
Preparation time: 10 minutes +
10 minutes chilling
Calories per serving: 205

Slice the top off a medium orange and hollow out. Keep the flesh to one side. Chop up a Weight Watchers Chocolate Crisp into small pieces and mix with one pot of Tesco, less-than-1%-fat, Chocolate Mousse (1½ Points). Add the orange flesh to this mixture and spoon back into the orange 'bowl'. Chill for 10 minutes before serving.

BANOFFEE POT

POINTS	per serving: 3

(V) *Serves 2*
Preparation time: 5 minutes
Calories per serving: 105

Chop a Weight Watchers Chocolate Crisp into small pieces and divide between two ramekin dishes. Top with a sliced medium banana and then divide a 120 g pot of Weight Watchers from Heinz Toffee Yogurt between the two dishes. To serve, top with a tablespoon of low-fat aerosal cream.

APPLE 'CRUMBLE'

POINTS	per serving: 2¹/₂

(V) *Serves 2*
Preparation and cooking time: 20 minutes
Calories per serving: 125

Divide one large cooked sliced cooking apple between two ramekins. Top each ramekin with half a crumbled Weight Watchers All Day Snack Bar. Cook in the oven at Gas Mark 4/180°C/350°F for 15 minutes and serve each with half a small pot (150 g) of ready-to-serve low-fat custard.

And now keep reading for more fabulous ideas from the people at the heart of Weight Watchers... our Members and Leaders!

Spicy Seafood Soup: Ideal for a special occasion at only 2 Points per serving!

We know you are always looking for something satisfying and soups are ideal. They can be very low in Points and sometimes totally Point-free which means you can fill up on them when you are feeling hungry. The starters are very adaptable so think of them as being suitable for snacks or packed lunches too.

SPICY SEAFOOD SOUP

POINTS

per recipe: 8½   per serving: 2

Serves 4
Preparation time: 15 minutes
Cooking time: 25 minutes
Calories per serving: 190
Freezing: not recommended

Jane Ferguson, a Member from Aberdeen, created this excellent fish recipe after she tried a spicy seafood soup in a Spanish tapas bar in Glasgow. She often serves it for a special Friday night supper with her husband. It goes down a treat with a (2.5 cm/1-inch) slice of garlic bread (1½ Points) or a medium slice of fresh crusty bread (1 Point) – and a glass (100 ml) of chilled white wine (1 Point).

low-fat cooking spray
1 onion, sliced
1 leek, sliced
1 garlic clove, chopped finely
400 g can of chopped tomatoes
300 ml (½ pint) white wine
1 fish or vegetable stock cube, dissolved in 425 ml (¾ pint) hot water
1 bouquet garni
1 tablespoon chopped fresh parsley plus extra to garnish
½ teaspoon dried dill weed (optional)
¼ teaspoon cayenne pepper
¼ teaspoon paprika
1 bay leaf
350 g (12 oz) frozen seafood cocktail
75 g (2¾ oz) cod or haddock fillet, cubed
100 g (3½ oz) mussels in shells, scrubbed
salt and freshly ground black pepper

1 Spray a large saucepan with two squirts of low-fat cooking spray. Heat for a few seconds, then add the onion, leek and garlic. Cook over a medium heat, stirring often, until the vegetables look transparent, but not browned, about 5–8 minutes.

2 Add the chopped tomatoes, white wine and stock. Stir in all the seasonings, except the salt and black pepper.

3 Tip in all the seafood, making sure that you discard any mussels that are damaged or open. Heat until just simmering, then reduce the heat to low and simmer gently for 10–15 minutes.

4 Discard any mussels that have failed to open and remove the bay leaf and bouquet garni. Check the seasoning, adding salt and pepper to taste. Ladle into warmed soup bowls and serve at once, garnished with extra chopped parsley.

TOP TIPS Jane keeps packs of frozen mixed seafood in her freezer, at the ready to make her delicious recipe. Most of the other ingredients are storecupboard items, so you only need to buy a few fresh vegetables, the fish and mussels.

Serve as a light meal for two instead of for four and the soup still has just 4 Points per serving.

ROOT AND ORANGE SOUP

POINTS

per recipe: ½   per serving: 0

V *Serves 6*

Preparation time: 15 minutes
Cooking time: 20 minutes
Calories per serving: 75
Freezing: recommended

Sue Coats is an enthusiastic Leader from near Warrington in Cheshire, taking three Meetings a week in Woolston. She enjoys cooking for her family, and loves to pass on tips to Members such as this delicious soup recipe that's totally Point-free.

500 g (1 lb 2 oz) carrots, diced

1 small swede, diced

2 red onions, chopped

1 garlic clove, crushed

2 vegetable stock cubes, dissolved in 1½ litres (2¾ pints) hot water

1 tablespoon tomato purée

1 tablespoon balsamic vinegar

finely grated zest and juice of 1 orange

1 tablespoon chopped fresh parsley or chives plus extra to garnish

salt and freshly ground black pepper

1 Put the carrots, swede, onions and garlic into a large saucepan.
2 Pour in the stock, tomato purée and balsamic vinegar. Stir well. Bring up to the boil, then reduce the heat to low and simmer gently for 15–20 minutes, until the vegetables are tender.
3 Leave the soup chunky or liquidise in a blender or food processor until smooth. Stir in the orange zest and juice with the parsley or chives and check the seasoning, adding salt and pepper, if needed.

4 Ladle the soup into warmed bowls and garnish with extra chopped parsley or chives.

TOP TIP For a special garnish, top each portion with a tablespoon of low-fat plain yogurt, some extra parsley or chives and a little more grated orange zest. This will not add any Points.

VARIATION Ring the changes with lemon zest and juice instead of orange, and change the vegetables according to their availability – for instance, use spring onions or shallots instead of red onions.

MULLIGATAWNY SOUP

POINTS

per recipe: 2   per serving: ½

V *if using vegetable stock cubes*
Serves 6
Preparation time: 20 minutes
Cooking time: 35 minutes
Calories per serving: 85
Freezing: recommended

Amanda Seddon is a Member who lives in Orrell, near Wigan in Lancashire. She recommends this soup for a tasty, low-Point lunch. Because she goes out to work, she takes a frozen portion of the soup with her, then reheats it at lunch time for a warming, satisfying light meal.

1 cooking apple, cored and chopped

2 medium carrots, chopped

2 leeks, sliced

1 onion, chopped

1 medium potato, diced

2 garlic cloves, crushed

1 tablespoon medium curry powder

400 g can of chopped tomatoes

2 vegetable or chicken stock cubes, dissolved in 1.2 litres (2 pints) hot water

salt and freshly ground black pepper

1 Put the apple and all the vegetables (except the tomatoes) into a large saucepan and add 3 tablespoons of cold water. Cook over a medium heat for about 5 minutes, until the onion looks transparent.
2 Add the garlic and curry powder and cook for 1 or 2 more minutes, adding a little extra water, if needed, to prevent sticking.

3 Add the tomatoes and stock to the saucepan. Bring up to the boil, then reduce the heat and simmer for 25–30 minutes until the vegetables are soft.
4 Transfer to a liquidiser or food processor and blend for about 15–20 seconds until smooth.
5 Return to the saucepan and reheat gently. Season to taste, then serve.

TOP TIPS For a fabulous finish, swirl 1 tablespoon of half-fat crème fraîche through each portion and sprinkle with chopped fresh coriander. This will add an extra ½ Point per serving.

If freezing, cool and freeze in six separate portions so you can be sure of having the right amount of Points in each serving.

Root and Orange Soup: It's too good to be true: this soup is full of flavour but entirely Point-free!

GARLIC SOUP

POINTS

per recipe: 7	per serving: $1^{1}/_{2}$

(V) *if using a vegetable stock cube*

Serves 4
Preparation time: 10 minutes
Cooking time: 30 minutes
Calories per serving: 155
Freezing: recommended

David Orde is a Member and retired head teacher from Bognor Regis in West Sussex. He enjoyed a superb garlic soup when travelling in Austria. As he couldn't find a similar recipe, he decided to develop his own, with Weight Watchers in mind. It tastes fantastic, and has a lovely velvety texture. And don't worry – it doesn't have a strong garlic flavour but is smooth and mellow!

1 tablespoon olive oil
1 large onion, chopped finely
1 large garlic bulb (about 8–10 cloves), split, peeled and sliced
225 g (8 oz) potatoes, diced
600 ml (1 pint) skimmed milk
1 vegetable or chicken stock cube, dissolved in 50 ml (2 fl oz) hot water
2 tablespoons chopped fresh mixed herbs (e.g. parsley, chives, marjoram)
salt and freshly ground black pepper

1 Gently heat the olive oil in a large saucepan. Add the onion, stir well, then cover and cook over a low heat for about 5 minutes to sweat gently.

2 Add the sliced garlic to the saucepan. Cover again and cook gently for another 5 minutes, stirring from time to time.

3 Add the potatoes and cook, stirring, for another minute. Next, add the milk and bring up to the boil, stirring all the time. Add the stock and herbs. Reduce the heat and simmer for 15–20 minutes, or until the potatoes are tender.

4 Blend the soup in a liquidiser or food processor until smooth and velvety. Return to the saucepan and reheat gently, then season to taste and serve.

TOP TIP If you don't have any fresh herbs to hand, use 1 rounded teaspoon of dried mixed herbs instead.

Butternut Squash Soup: Delicious, thick, satisfying and there are no Points!

BUTTERNUT SQUASH SOUP

POINTS

per recipe: 0	per serving: 0

(V) Serves 2
Preparation time: 10 minutes
Cooking time: 20 minutes
Calories per serving: 155
Freezing: recommended

This delicious zero Point soup couldn't be simpler to make. It was devised by Gail Burns, a Member from Kirkby-in-Furness in Cumbria, where she has two important roles in the community: a Deaconess at a local village church and a lollipop lady!

1 small butternut squash, peeled, de-seeded and chopped
1 onion, chopped
1 vegetable stock cube, dissolved in 600 ml (1 pint) hot water
salt and freshly ground black pepper

1 Put the squash and onion into a large saucepan and add the stock.

2 Bring up to the boil, then reduce the heat and simmer for about 20 minutes until the squash is tender.

3 Transfer the soup to a liquidiser or food processor and blend until smooth.

4 Return to the saucepan and reheat gently. Season to taste, then serve.

TOP TIP For four servings, use a medium to large butternut squash, a large onion, 2 stock cubes and 850 ml (1½ pints) hot water.

VARIATIONS When in season, you can make this soup with pumpkin instead of squash.

For a spicy flavour, try adding a good pinch of ground cumin and ground coriander to the soup with the stock. Garnish with chopped fresh coriander or parsley.

CELERY, APPLE AND TOMATO SOUP

POINTS

per recipe: 4   per serving: ½

(V) Serves 8
Preparation time: 10 minutes
Cooking time: 50 minutes
Calories per serving: 70
Freezing: recommended

Lynn Soules, a Gold Member from Hoo near Rochester in Kent, invented this tasty soup when she wanted a low-Point starter for Christmas. It became a family favourite, so now she serves it all year round. It freezes brilliantly, so make the full amount and freeze what you don't need.

low-fat cooking spray
1 head of celery, trimmed and chopped
2 onions, chopped
2 leeks, chopped
2 cooking apples, chopped
2 vegetable stock cubes, dissolved in 850 ml (1½ pints) hot water
300 ml (½ pint) unsweetened apple juice
2 × 400 g cans tomatoes
2 tablespoons chopped fresh parsley
1 teaspoon caster sugar
salt and freshly ground black pepper

1 Spray a large saucepan with 2–3 squirts of low-fat cooking spray. Heat for a few seconds, then add the celery, onions and leeks. Cook over a medium-low heat, stirring often, for about 8–10 minutes.

2 Add the apples, stock, apple juice and tomatoes and bring up to the boil. Reduce the heat and simmer gently for 40 minutes.

3 Transfer the soup to a liquidiser or food processor and blend until smooth. Return to the saucepan and add the parsley and caster sugar. Reheat gently, season to taste, then serve.

TOP TIPS This soup is really delicious when partially liquidised, so that it has a smooth consistency with a chunky texture. Simply blend about two thirds of the soup for 15–20 seconds, then return it to the saucepan with the reserved amount.

Celery leaves make a great garnish – just chop roughly and sprinkle over the soup.

COTTAGE CHEESE PEACHES

POINTS

per recipe: 2½   per serving: ½

(V) if using vegetarian cottage cheese
Serves 4
Preparation time: 10 minutes
Calories per serving: 40
Freezing: not recommended

Valerie Stoddart is the Leader for two Meetings held at Alford and Aboyne in Aberdeenshire. As well as being a mum to three young children, she works part-time for a design agency. She loves to cook, and has created an easy, refreshing starter.

shredded lettuce leaves
4 canned peach halves in natural juice, drained
110 g tub of low-fat cottage cheese with pineapple
paprika, for sprinkling
a few slices of cucumber
2 tomatoes, sliced or 8 cherry tomatoes, halved
2 spring onions, chopped finely
chopped fresh parsley, to garnish

1 Arrange the shredded lettuce leaves on four serving plates or in the base of four bowls. Top each one with half a peach, cut-side uppermost.

2 Fill the cavity of each peach with an equal amount of cottage cheese. Sprinkle with paprika.

3 Garnish with cucumber slices and tomatoes, then sprinkle with the spring onions and chopped parsley.

TOP TIPS When fresh peaches or nectarines are available, use them as an alternative to the canned peach halves.

If you're having a party, the peaches are an attractive, low-Point addition to a buffet spread and they're so easy to assemble.

Creamy Garlic Mushrooms: The flavour is heavenly and only ½ Point per serving.

CREAMY GARLIC MUSHROOMS

POINTS

per recipe: 2½	per serving: ½

V if using vegetarian cheese

Serves 4

Preparation time: 5 minutes

Cooking time: 7–8 minutes

Calories per serving: 55

Freezing: not recommended

Valerie Batty, a Gold Member, is a pedicare therapist from the pretty town of Oakham in Rutland. As a Gold Member since 1995, she has perfected this marvellous mushroom recipe. It's ideal for enjoying as a starter without over-doing the Points.

4 large flat mushrooms, wiped

100 g (3½ oz) low-fat soft cheese

2 garlic cloves, crushed or finely chopped

1 tablespoon chopped fresh parsley

2–3 teaspoons skimmed milk

salt and freshly ground black pepper

1 Trim the mushroom stalks, then arrange the mushrooms, stalk side down, on a large microwaveable plate. Microwave on HIGH for 3 minutes.

2 Meanwhile, preheat the grill.

3 Put the soft cheese into a mixing bowl and add the garlic, parsley and milk, beating until smooth and creamy.

4 Turn the mushrooms over and divide the soft cheese mixture between them. Level off the surface, season, then grill until lightly browned and bubbling. Serve at once.

TOP TIP If you don't have a microwave, poach the mushrooms in a little stock or water in a large frying-pan for about 4–5 minutes. Drain well, then fill and grill as above.

VARIATION The creamy garlic mixture can be added to thinly sliced poached mushrooms, then used as a filling for a jacket potatoes, remembering to add 2½ Points per medium potato for a delicious lunch.

POTTED PEPPERED MACKEREL

POINTS

per recipe: 14½	per serving: 2½

Serves 6

Preparation time: 10 minutes

Calories per serving: 145

Freezing: recommended

Julia Wood, a Member from Fulwood near Preston in Lancashire, is a full-time mum. Her tasty mackerel pâté is a lunch time favourite. Serve with salad and a medium jacket potato (add 2½ Points each) or with toast (as pictured).

220 g can of butter beans, drained

200 g (7 oz) peppered mackerel fillets, skinned

1 large red onion, chopped very finely

1 garlic clove, crushed (optional)

finely grated zest and juice of 1 lemon

1 tablespoon chopped fresh parsley

salt and freshly ground black pepper

TO GARNISH

parsley sprigs

lemon slices

1 Tip the drained beans into a large mixing bowl and use a potato masher or fork to mash to a purée.

2 Add the mackerel fillets and flake roughly with a fork, then stir into the beans.

3 Add most of the red onion, reserving a little for garnish. Add the garlic (if using), lemon zest, lemon juice and parsley. Season, then mix together thoroughly.

4 Divide the mixture between six small ramekin dishes. Cover and chill until ready to serve, then garnish with parsley sprigs, lemon slices and the reserved red onion.

TOP TIPS If you prefer, use a drained 190 g can of peppered mackerel instead.

For a smooth pâté, whizz together all the ingredients in a food processor or blender for 15 seconds.

VARIATIONS Canned chick-peas or cannellini beans can be used instead of butter beans. These are best when puréed in a blender. The Points will be the same.

For a decorative starter that doesn't add further Points, use the mackerel pâté to fill hollowed-out tomatoes.

Potted Peppered Mackerel: With two medium slices of toast, the Points per serving will be 4½.

BAKED TUNA PÂTÉ

POINTS

per recipe: 10½   per serving: 2½

Serves 4
Preparation time: 10 minutes
Cooking time: 30 minutes
Calories per serving: 160
Freezing: not recommended

Del Berwick is a Leader from Rothwell in Northamptonshire. She serves this unusual pâté as a starter or a snack with salad and two extra-thin crispbreads per person (add ½ Point) or 6 small Melba toasts per person (add 1 Point). The recipe was originally made for her by a friend as a dinner party starter, and Del has made it ever since.

15 g (½ oz) polyunsaturated margarine
50 g (1¾ oz) onion, finely chopped
50 g (1¾ oz) mushrooms, finely chopped
200 g can of tuna in brine, drained and flaked
25 g (1 oz) fresh wholemeal breadcrumbs
150 g (5½ oz) low-fat plain yogurt
1 tablespoon tomato purée
1 egg yolk
3 tablespoons single cream
salt and freshly ground black pepper

1 Preheat the oven to Gas Mark 4/180°C/350°F.

2 Melt the margarine in a frying-pan and sauté the onion and mushrooms for about 3–4 minutes, until softened. Remove from the heat.

3 Combine all the remaining ingredients together in a mixing bowl. Add the onion and mushrooms, mix well, then divide between four ramekin dishes or individual ovenproof serving dishes.

4 Stand the dishes on a baking sheet, then bake for 20–25 minutes. Leave to cool, then serve.

VARIATION If you like canned salmon, try it as an alternative to tuna. Use pink or red salmon; the Points per serving will be 4.

PASTA COCKTAIL

POINTS

per recipe: 9   per serving: 1½

 Serves 6
Preparation time: 10 minutes
Cooking time: 12 minutes
Calories per serving: 105
Freezing: not recommended

Tracy Roberts is a Member from Dumfries in Scotland. She loves pasta, so she developed this refreshing starter which combines crunchy no-Point vegetables with crisp apple in a delicious dressing. You can also serve it as a great accompaniment to a medium skinless grilled chicken breast for a total of 4 Points.

75 g (2¾ oz) dried pasta shapes
4 tablespoons low-fat mayonnaise
2 tablespoons tomato sauce
2 tablespoons low-fat plain yogurt
2 teaspoons lemon juice
a dash of Tabasco sauce
3 celery sticks, chopped
1 red or yellow pepper, de-seeded and chopped
10 cm (4-inch) piece of cucumber, chopped
1 red apple, cored and chopped
a few crisp lettuce leaves, shredded
salt and freshly ground black pepper
lemon wedges, to garnish

1 Cook the pasta in plenty of lightly salted boiling water for 10–12 minutes, or according to pack instructions. Drain well and rinse with cold water to cool.

2 In a large bowl, mix together the mayonnaise, tomato sauce, yogurt, lemon juice and Tabasco.

3 Tip the pasta into the sauce and add the celery, pepper, cucumber and apple. Season lightly, then mix together gently.

4 Line six cocktail glasses or serving dishes with shredded lettuce, then fill with the pasta mixture. Garnish with lemon wedges, then serve.

TOP TIP If you like, add a tablespoon of chopped fresh herbs to the mixture; mint, chives or parsley all taste delicious in this recipe.

VARIATION Vary the vegetables according to your personal preferences. Radishes, tomatoes, cucumber and red onion make a tasty combination and are all Point-free additions.

**Pasta Cocktail:
A very versatile
recipe with
a delicious
refreshing
flavour and only
1½ Points per
serving.**

Rosti Fish Cakes: A novel idea for cooking with fish and well worth the effort! Only 2½ Points per serving.

light meals & snacks

What a creative lot you are! Some very tasty little numbers fill these pages. From reading your recipes, it's clear that more and more of you are enjoying food that's full of delicious flavours, colours and textures. And you love to experiment with new and different ingredients to keep the taste buds interested whilst the body gets into shape.

So, no boring restrictive diets for you! It's clear that you relish tasty, satisfying, flavoursome food that means that you enjoy every mouthful. So tuck in to these superb recipes for light meals, salads, snacks and side dishes.

ROSTI FISH CAKES

POINTS	
per recipe: **10**	per serving: **2½**

Serves 4
Preparation and cooking time:
45 minutes
Calories per serving: 190
Freezing: not recommended

Jane Goodwin, a Gold Member from Melton Constable in Norfolk, has devised this tasty recipe. She works in a delicatessen, so is surrounded by delicious food all day long – not easy when you're trying to lose weight! Point-free salad or vegetables are perfect accompaniments to these fish cakes.

300 g (10½ oz) new potatoes, unpeeled
400 g can of tuna in brine, drained
½ teaspoon finely grated lime zest
1 tablespoon lime juice
a dash of soy sauce
2 tablespoons sweet chilli sauce
2 tablespoons finely chopped red onion
2 tablespoons chopped fresh coriander
low-fat cooking spray
4 tablespoons Weight Watchers from Heinz Mayonnaise-style Dressing, to serve

1 Cook the new potatoes in lightly salted boiling water for 15–20 minutes, until tender.
2 Meanwhile, put the drained tuna in a bowl with the lime zest and juice, soy sauce and chilli sauce. Add the onion and coriander and mix together.
3 Cool the cooked potatoes for about 10 minutes, then grate coarsely, trying to make the strips as long as possible. Combine with the tuna mixture, form into eight cakes, then chill in the fridge.

4 Heat a large frying-pan and add 2–3 sprays of the low-fat cooking spray. Cook the cakes for approximately 4 minutes on each side, until golden brown. Serve two cakes per portion, with a tablespoon of the mayonnaise.

TOP TIP Only use the coloured part of the lime zest. Avoid the white pith as this will add a bitter taste.

VARIATIONS Use any cooked white fish for this recipe and the Points will remain the same, or try 400 g canned red salmon, which will make the Points 4 per serving.

Vegetarians could omit the fish altogether to make lime and coriander rosti potato cakes (1½ Points per serving).

Use lemon zest and lemon juice instead of lime, if you prefer.

COLOURFUL COUSCOUS CASSEROLE

POINTS

per recipe: 14   per serving: 2½

 Serves 6

Preparation time: 20 minutes

Cooking time: 40–45 minutes

Calories per serving: 255

Freezing: not recommended

Rachel Wells is a Member from
Scarborough in North Yorkshire,
and says this recipe has really helped
her to lose weight. It's a brilliant dish
for feeding friends and it's suitable
for vegetarians and vegans too.

250 g (9 oz) couscous

1 teaspoon olive oil

125 ml (4 fl oz) boiling water

2 large onions, chopped

*1 vegetable stock cube, dissolved in
125 ml (4 fl oz) hot water*

3 or 4 garlic cloves, crushed

2 leeks, sliced

*1 red, 1 green and 1 yellow pepper,
de-seeded and sliced*

*100 g (3½ oz) broccoli, broken into
florets*

8 mushrooms, wiped and sliced

150 g (5½ oz) baby corn

2 × 400 g cans of chopped tomatoes

6 tomatoes, sliced

salt and freshly ground black pepper

parsley sprigs, to garnish (optional)

1 Put the couscous into a large
mixing bowl and add the olive oil
and boiling water, stirring to mix.
Cover and leave for 5 minutes.

2 Preheat the oven to Gas Mark 3/
170°C/320°F.

3 Put the onions, stock and garlic into
a frying-pan and cook for 5 minutes.

4 Stir the onion mixture into the
couscous with all the remaining
vegetables and chopped tomatoes,
but not the sliced fresh tomatoes.
Season well with salt and pepper.

5 Transfer the couscous mixture to
a large ovenproof dish and arrange
the sliced tomatoes on top. Cover
with a lid or a piece of foil and
bake for 30–40 minutes.

6 Remove the lid, garnish with
parsley, if using, then serve.

VARIATIONS For a main meal,
top the couscous with a grilled or
baked medium-sized cod steak and
garnish with watercress. This will
add a ½ Point per serving. Any
leftovers? Serve them cold as a salad.

Vary the Point-free vegetables
according to the season and your
own preferences.

GARLIC BAKED POTATOES

POINTS

per recipe: 11½   per serving: 3

Serves 4

Preparation time: 10 minutes

Cooking time: 1–1¼ hours

Calories per serving: 190

Freezing: not recommended

Diane Slender is a Member who
lives in Upper Sundon near Luton
in Bedfordshire. She loves potatoes,
and has come up with the idea of
serving them in this delicious way –
a cross between roast and baked,
without the Points.

4 medium baking potatoes

2 garlic cloves, cut into thin slivers

*4 tablespoons very low-fat
fromage frais*

4 tablespoons low-fat plain yogurt

2 tablespoons chopped fresh chives

*6–8 watercress sprigs, finely chopped
plus extra, to garnish*

salt and freshly ground black pepper

1 Preheat the oven to Gas Mark 6/
200°C/400°F.

2 Slice each potato at approximately
5 mm (¼-inch) intervals, cutting not
quite through to the base, so that
they retain their shape. Slip slivers
of garlic between the cuts in the
potatoes.

3 Put the potatoes in a roasting dish
or on a baking sheet and bake for
1–1¼ hours. Then check with a sharp
knife to make sure they are tender.

4 Meanwhile, mix together the
fromage frais, yogurt, chives and
chopped watercress. Season with a
little salt and pepper, then cover
and chill until ready to serve.

5 Serve the potatoes with a dollop
of the herb mixture and garnish with
watercress sprigs.

TOP TIP With a large Point-free
salad, this makes a delicious light
meal. Alternatively, serve the potatoes
with a grilled medium skinless
chicken breast adding 2½ Points per
serving or a medium-sized cod fillet
adding 1 Point per serving.

Colourful Couscous Casserole: Bring the entire dish to the table as seen here and let everyone dig in for only 2½ Points per serving.

SIMPLY QUICHE

POINTS

per recipe: $7^1/_2$ per serving: $3^1/_2$

Serves 2
Preparation time: 10 minutes
Cooking time: 15–20 minutes
Calories per serving: 230
Freezing: recommended

Sheila Young is an ex-primary school teacher from Fleetwood in Lancashire, and since becoming a Member, she has improved both her health and her outline! This is her scrumptious version of Quiche Lorraine, with far fewer Points than the original version. Serve hot or cold with a Point-free salad or vegetable.

2 medium slices bread
2 teaspoons low-fat spread
1 rasher lean back bacon
1 egg, beaten
small tub (110 g) of diet cottage cheese
1 tablespoon finely chopped onion
salt and freshly ground black pepper

1 Preheat the oven to Gas Mark 6/ 200°C/400°F.
2 Flatten the slices of bread with a rolling pin until thin, then spread with the low-fat spread. Use the slices (spread side up) to line a small flan case, about 14 cm (5½ inches) in diameter.
3 Grill the bacon rasher until crisp, then snip into small pieces. Mix with the egg, cottage cheese and onion. Season with a little salt and pepper.
4 Pour the mixture into the bread-lined flan case. Bake in the centre of the oven until set, about 20 minutes.

TOP TIP For individual portions, cook the quiche in Yorkshire pudding tins or tartlet tins.

VARIATIONS Use 4–5 chopped spring onions instead of the onion.

If you are vegetarian, omit the bacon and use some chopped vegetables instead – courgettes and peppers would be ideal. The Points per serving will be 3.

**Marmite Chips:
The tastiest
chips ever!**

MARMITE CHIPS

POINTS

per recipe: 7   per serving: $3^1/_2$

(V) Serves 2
Preparation time: 10 minutes
Cooking time: 30–35 minutes
Calories per serving: 280
Freezing: not recommended

Leann Goral is a Leader from Huddersfield in West Yorkshire. Before becoming a Leader she lost 3 stone, and loves **pure points**™ since she can eat plenty and still lose weight. As she says to her Members 'Don't eat less, eat more wisely'.

500 g (1 lb 2 oz) potatoes, peeled
2 teaspoons vegetable oil
2 teaspoons Marmite
salt and freshly ground black pepper

1 Slice the potatoes into 1 cm (½-inch) wedges or chunky chips. Place in a saucepan of water, bring up to the boil, then reduce the heat and simmer for about 8 minutes, until just beginning to cook on the outside.
2 Preheat the oven to Gas Mark 7/ 220°C/425°F.
3 Drain the potatoes thoroughly, allowing them to steam for 1 or 2 minutes to dry off.
4 Add the oil and Marmite to the hot potatoes in the saucepan. Cover and shake the pan for a few moments to coat the potatoes, then tip them on to a baking sheet lined with baking parchment. Season.
5 Bake for 20–25 minutes until crisp and golden, turning once after 10 minutes.

TOP TIP To make a tasty dip, mix together 4 tablespoons of low-fat mayonnaise with 4 tablespoons of low-fat plain yogurt. Flavour with wholegrain mustard, Worcestershire sauce, chopped fresh herbs or spices. This will be 6 Points per serving, including the chips.

LAMB KOFTAS WITH MINT DIP

POINTS

per recipe: 27   per serving: 3½

Serves 8
Preparation time: 15 minutes
Cooking time: 10–15 minutes
Calories per serving: 145
Freezing: recommended (koftas only)

Sue Wynne is a real foodie from Widnes in Cheshire. As a Gold Member she puts her creative talents into thinking up healthy, tasty, low-Point dishes. This is one of them!

---
500 g (1 lb 2 oz) lean minced lamb

---
1 garlic clove, crushed

¼ teaspoon chilli powder

---
1 tablespoon chopped fresh coriander

---
1 tablespoon chopped fresh mint

---
1 egg, beaten

---
a dash of Tabasco sauce

---
25 g (1 oz) branflakes, crushed

---
1 teaspoon salt

FOR THE DIP
250 g (9 oz) tub of Quark

---
a dash of Tabasco sauce

---
1 teaspoon lemon juice

---
1 teaspoon lime juice

---
1 teaspoon mint sauce or 1 tablespoon chopped fresh mint

---
grated zest of lemon and lime

---

1 Preheat the grill.
2 Mix together all the kofta ingredients, then divide into 8 equal portions. Form into long sausage shapes around 8 metal skewers or bamboo sticks.

3 Grill for 10–15 minutes, turning frequently, until well-browned and thoroughly cooked.
4 Combine all the ingredients for the dip together until smooth and creamy. Serve with the koftas.

TOP TIP If using bamboo skewers, soak them in hot water for about 10 minutes before use, to prevent them from burning.

VARIATION For less Points, use minced turkey instead of lamb. Serve with a garlic dip, made by omitting the mint, lime zest and juice and replacing them with a crushed garlic clove and some chopped fresh parsley. The Points per serving will be 2.

SALMON AND AVOCADO JACKETS

POINTS

per recipe: 19   per serving: 4½

Serves 4
Preparation time: 5 minutes
Cooking time: 1 hour
Calories per serving: 290
Freezing: not recommended

For a quick and tasty filling for jacket potatoes, Mrs Hallin, a Gold Member from Southsea in Hampshire, whizzes together a few ingredients in her blender and the result is a very tasty light lunch or supper dish.

---
4 medium baking potatoes

---
100 g (3½ oz) smoked salmon trimmings

½ medium avocado

---
200 g can of tuna in brine or water, drained

---
2 teaspoons balsamic vinegar

---
25 g (1 oz) Quark

---
freshly ground black pepper

---
chopped fresh parsley or coriander, to garnish

---

1 Preheat the oven to Gas Mark 6/ 200°C/400°F.
2 Bake the potatoes for approximately 1 hour, until tender.
3 A few minutes before the potatoes are ready, put the salmon trimmings, avocado, tuna, vinegar and Quark into a food processor or blender and whizz together for a few seconds until smooth. Season to taste with a little black pepper.

4 Make a deep cut in the top of the potatoes, push open and fill with an equal amount of the filling. Serve at once, garnished with chopped fresh parsley or coriander.

TOP TIP For a chunkier texture, simply mix together all the filling ingredients with a fork.

VARIATIONS You can use lemon or lime juice instead of balsamic vinegar, if you prefer.

Instead of using the avocado mixture to fill jacket potatoes, serve with 2 medium slices of hot toast per person. The Points per serving will be 4.

HADDOCK RAREBIT

POINTS

per recipe: 11½   per serving: 5½

Serves 2
Preparation time: 15 minutes
Cooking time: 15 minutes
Calories per serving: 380
Freezing: not recommended

Judith Warrington is a Member and retired TV Producer from Battle in East Sussex. She loves this nourishing, low-Point fish dish which is perfect for a light lunch or supper. She hopes other Members will enjoy it too.

2 × 200 g (7 oz) smoked haddock fillets
400 g (14 oz) frozen chopped spinach
75 g (2¾ oz) half-fat Cheddar cheese, grated
2 tablespoons low-fat mayonnaise
½ teaspoon mustard powder
1 teaspoon Worcestershire sauce
shake of Tabasco sauce
½ teaspoon grated nutmeg
salt and freshly ground black pepper

1 Put the haddock fillets into a non-stick frying-pan and add 200 ml (⅓ pint) water. Poach gently for about 6–8 minutes until the fish is cooked; the flesh should be opaque and flake easily.
2 Meanwhile, cook the spinach according to pack instructions, squeeze out the excess moisture, then transfer to two individual shallow heatproof dishes. Season with a little salt and pepper.
3 Remove the skin from the haddock, then lay one fillet on top of the spinach in each dish.
4 Preheat the grill.
5 Mix the cheese with the mayonnaise, mustard, Worcestershire sauce, Tabasco sauce and nutmeg. Spread this mixture over the fish fillets to cover them completely. Grill until browned and bubbling, then serve at once.

TOP TIP The dish can be finished off in the oven instead of under the grill. Simply bake for about 5–6 minutes at Gas Mark 6/200°C/400°F.

VARIATION For a 'Buck Haddock Rarebit', add a poached egg and serve it on top of the fish and cheese, remembering to add 1½ Points per serving.

SPICY SWEDE RATATOUILLE

POINTS

per recipe: 2   per serving: ½

 Serves 4
Preparation time: 15 minutes
Cooking time: 1½ hours
Calories per serving: 110
Freezing: recommended

Margaret Beaman is a Member from Kings Langley in Hertfordshire. Her recipe is a tasty filler, perfect for when you know you are going to eat out later. As Margaret says 'Save Points – yes! But eat less – no! Arrive at your "do" with plenty of Points left, but able to resist going overboard because you've eaten well beforehand.'

1 swede, peeled and cut into chunks
500 g (1 lb 2 oz) passata or creamed tomatoes
1 onion, chopped
500 g (1 lb 2 oz) mushrooms, sliced
2 courgettes, sliced
2 garlic cloves, crushed
1 small red chilli, de-seeded and chopped finely
2 teaspoons grated fresh root ginger
salt and freshly ground black pepper

1 Preheat the oven to Gas Mark 4/ 180°C/350°F.
2 Cook the swede in lightly salted boiling water for about 10 minutes, until almost tender. Drain well.
3 Put the swede into a large casserole dish with the passata or creamed tomatoes. Add all the other ingredients and stir together. Season with salt and pepper.
4 Cover and cook in the oven for 1¼–1½ hours.

TOP TIP For a main course, serve it on a medium portion (150 g/5½ oz) of cooked rice (adding 3 Points per serving), or have it as a side dish with fish or meat, not forgetting to add the extra Points.

VARIATION Use 2 medium potatoes instead of the swede. This will increase the Points to 1 per serving.

Haddock Rarebit: This quick and easy fish dish is full of delicious and comforting flavours and only 5½ Points per serving.

Roasted Vegetable Bagels: The gorgeous flavour of roasted vegetables is so hard to beat and only 4 Points per serving!

ROASTED VEGETABLE BAGELS

POINTS

per recipe: 8   **per serving:** 4

Ⓥ *if using vegetarian cheese*

Serves 2

Preparation time: 15 minutes
+ cooling

Cooking time: 5 minutes

Calories per serving: 280

Freezing: not recommended

Shuba Singhal is a Member and junior doctor from Didsbury, Manchester. She makes these delicious bagels to take to work with her since she says that healthy vegetarian options aren't always available in the shops or as tasty!

low-fat cooking spray

½ red pepper, de-seeded and sliced into 4 pieces

½ yellow or green pepper, de-seeded and sliced into 4 pieces

½ small courgette, sliced thinly

4 thin slices of aubergine (optional)

a few fresh basil leaves, torn into pieces

2 tablespoons balsamic vinegar

a dash of Tabasco sauce (optional)

2 medium bagels

75 g (2¾ oz) low-fat soft cheese

salt and freshly ground black pepper

1 Heat a griddle pan or frying-pan until hot, then add 2–3 sprays of low-fat cooking spray.

2 Put the peppers, courgette and aubergine (if using) into the pan. Cook for about 5 minutes, turning often until well done, and pressing the vegetables down with a spatula to char them.

3 Tip the vegetables into a bowl and add the basil and balsamic vinegar. Season with salt and pepper, add a dash of Tabasco sauce if liked, then mix well. Cover and leave to cool.

4 Slice the bagels in half and lightly toast the cut sides. Divide the low-fat soft cheese and spread evenly over both halves of each bagel. Arrange the prepared vegetables over one half, sandwich together, then serve.

TOP TIP Soften the vegetables in the microwave for 2 minutes on HIGH before roasting in the pan.

VARIATION Instead of low-fat soft cheese, use 1 tablespoon of reduced-fat hummous per bagel. The Points will be the same.

RED HOT PRAWN PITTAS

POINTS

per recipe: 6½   **per serving:** 3

Serves 2

Preparation time: 5 minutes

Cooking time: 2 minutes

Calories per serving: 250

Freezing: not recommended

Dianne Hopwood is a Leader from Bognor Regis in Sussex. She loves riding her motorbike, although it was one thing she couldn't do before she became a Member. So now she keeps trim, helped along by this delicious recipe.

2 medium pitta breads

low-fat cooking spray

½ red onion, sliced thinly

100 g (3½ oz) stir-fry vegetables

½ red pepper, de-seeded and sliced thinly

75 g (2¾ oz) prawns, defrosted if frozen

1½ tablespoons sweet chilli sauce

salt and freshly ground black pepper

1 Heat a wok or frying-pan until very hot. At the same time, warm the pitta breads in a toaster or under the grill.

2 Add 2–3 sprays of the low-fat cooking spray to the wok or frying-pan, then add the onion and stir-fry for a few seconds.

3 Add the stir-fry vegetables and red pepper and cook for another minute or two, stirring all the time.

4 Add the prawns and stir-fry for another few moments to heat through. Stir in the chilli sauce, season with salt and pepper, then stuff into the warmed pitta bread. Serve at once.

VARIATIONS Use the stir-fry mixture to fill lightly toasted bagels or medium baked potatoes, adjusting the Points to 4 for bagels or 3 for potatoes.

If you're vegetarian, omit the prawns and use 75 g (2¾ oz) of drained canned chick-peas instead. The Points will be 3½ per serving.

BROSTER SPECIAL

POINTS

per recipe: 3½   per serving: 3½

Ⓥ *Serves 1*
Preparation time: 5 minutes
Cooking time: 2–3 minutes
Calories per serving: 235
Freezing: not recommended

Jean Broster is a Member and practice nurse from Greasby on the Wirral. She enjoys this quick recipe as breakfast or dessert.

1 medium slice bread
1 teaspoon honey
1 small ripe banana
2 teaspoons half-fat crème fraîche
2 teaspoons fruit compote (apple, blackberry, strawberry or raspberry)

1 Preheat the grill, then toast the bread on both sides.

2 Drizzle the toast with the honey and top with sliced banana. Spread the crème fraîche lightly over the bananas, then drizzle the fruit compote over the top.

3 Grill until warm, but not browned.

TOP TIP Serve without grilling the top, if you like – it's just as nice!

SAINTLY EGG

POINTS

per recipe: 5½   per serving: 5½

Serves 1
Preparation time: 5 minutes
Cooking time: 5 minutes
Calories per serving: 335
Freezing: not recommended

Wendy Kerr is a busy mum from the seaside town of Newquay in Cornwall. She first became a Member in Australia and when she joined here, she was newly inspired by her enthusiastic Leader. She cooks herself this special light lunch to keep her on track.

1 egg
1 medium slice of bread
1 cheese triangle
2 tablespoons Weight Watchers from Heinz Mild Mustard Dressing
2 tablespoons semi-skimmed milk
4 wafer-thin slices ham
1 tablespoon half-fat Cheddar cheese, grated
salt and freshly ground black pepper

1 Boil or poach the egg and toast the bread.

2 In a microwaveable jug or bowl, mix the cheese triangle with the mustard dressing and milk. Microwave on HIGH for 1 minute, stirring after 30 seconds.

3 Place the ham on top of the toast, then top with the boiled or poached egg.

4 Cover with the hot cheese sauce mixture and sprinkle with the grated cheese. Season with salt and pepper, then serve.

TOP TIP If you don't have a microwave for step 2, heat the cheese triangle, mustard dressing and milk in a small saucepan until melted and smooth.

VARIATION For a lower Point alternative, use 4–6 lightly cooked asparagus spears instead of the egg. The Points per serving will be 4.

 FRUIT AND NUT BITES

POINTS

per recipe: 20½   per serving: 1

Ⓥ *Makes 20 slices*
Preparation time: 10 minutes +
2 hours standing time
Calories per slice: 60
Freezing: not recommended

Anne Wilkinson, a Member from Harrogate in North Yorkshire, is a retired Health Visitor. She developed this recipe from one originally created for her children as a healthier alternative to real sweets.

50 g (1¾ oz) dried mango slices
100 g (3½ oz) blanched almonds
75 g (2¾ oz) raisins
175 g (6 oz) ready-to-eat dried apricots
1 tablespoon cocoa powder
1 tablespoon cold tea
approximately 4 sheets of rice paper

1 In a blender or food processor, blend together the mango slices, almonds, raisins, apricots, cocoa and cold tea.

2 Divide the mixture into two, and place between sheets of rice paper, levelling the mixture out by hand, then flattening and spreading out with a rolling pin, so that the mixture is about 5 mm (¼-inch) thick.

3 Leave for about 2 hours, then cut into pieces with a sharp knife or scissors to make 20 bites.

4 Store in an airtight container.

TOP TIP Rice paper can be bought from supermarkets and good kitchenware suppliers. It is edible.

Fruit and Nut
Bites: Each
slice is only
1 Point.

Spicy Turkey Marrow: Perfect as the main dish for lunch or supper at only 2 Points per serving.

Here is a wealth of delicious dishes, just waiting to make an appearance on your dinner plate. So there's no need to say that you long for something different, just decide to cook it!

All the recipes in this book have been developed by fellow Members and Leaders of Weight Watchers, so they know a thing or two about how to keep their taste buds satisfied – without seeing the results go straight from their lips to their hips.

Here you'll find some dishy fish numbers, meat and poultry recipes – and some vegetarian ideas too – so there's something to suit all tastes.

SPICY TURKEY MARROW

POINTS

per recipe: 8½   per serving: 2

Ⓥ *if following the variation*
Serves 4
Preparation time: 25 minutes
Cooking time: 30–35 minutes
Calories per serving: 175
Freezing: not recommended

Dawn White is a Member from St Olaves in Norfolk. She enjoys good food and she also enjoys cooking it for her family. This dish is stuffed with a tasty turkey mixture which makes it filling and healthy. It's perfect for a lunch or supper dish.

1 medium marrow, halved lengthways and seeds removed
2 teaspoons vegetable oil
1 onion, chopped
1 carrot, grated
1 red pepper, de-seeded and chopped
2 garlic cloves, crushed
1 tablespoon mild curry powder or mixed spice
275 g (9½ oz) turkey mince
2 tablespoons chopped fresh herbs (or 1 tablespoon of dried)
1 tablespoon soy sauce
1 chicken stock cube, dissolved in 150 ml (¼ pint) hot water
2 tablespoons half-fat crème fraîche
salt and freshly ground black pepper

1 Preheat the oven to Gas Mark 6/ 200°C/400°F. Place the marrow in a large baking dish or roasting tin, cut sides uppermost.
2 Heat the vegetable oil in a large saucepan, add the onion and sauté gently for 2–3 minutes. Add the carrot, red pepper and garlic and cook gently for another 3–4 minutes, until softened. Stir in the curry powder or mixed spice and cook for 1 more minute.
3 Stir the turkey mince into the vegetables and add the herbs and soy sauce. Cook for 2–3 minutes over a medium-high heat, then add the chicken stock. Heat until boiling, then reduce the heat and simmer for about 10 minutes until the stock has been reduced by half. Season to taste with salt and pepper. Remove from the heat and stir in the crème fraîche.
4 Spoon the turkey mixture into the hollowed-out marrow. Add about 150 ml (¼ pint) of cold water to the baking dish or tin, then cover with foil and bake for 30–35 minutes, until the marrow is tender.

TOP TIP If you enjoy spicy food, add a little more curry powder and a generous dash of Tabasco sauce to the turkey mixture, at no extra Points.

VARIATION For a vegetarian meal, replace the turkey with a good selection of Point-free vegetables such as mushrooms, aubergine, celery, asparagus, mange-tout peas and green beans and use a vegetable stock cube instead of chicken. The Points per serving will be reduced to ½.

THAI SALMON SURPRISE

POINTS

per recipe: 14   per serving: 3½

Serves 4
Preparation time: 15 minutes
Cooking time: 25 minutes
Calories per serving: 255
Freezing: recommended (see step 3 and Top Tip)

Hazel Ross, a Gold Member from Great Rissington in Gloucestershire, developed this recipe after a trip to Thailand. It's very tasty and low in Points and ideal for a special occasion. Serve with a green salad or with a medium portion (200 g/7 oz) of cooked noodles, which will make the total Points per serving 6½.

1 small onion, chopped finely
2 cm (¾-inch) piece of lemon grass, chopped finely
2 cm (¾-inch) piece of fresh ginger, peeled and chopped finely
50 g (1¾ oz) mushrooms, chopped finely
½ red pepper, de-seeded and chopped finely
½ teaspoon Thai seven spice seasoning
1 tablespoon tomato purée
1 tablespoon chopped fresh coriander
4 × 125 g (4½ oz) thick-cut salmon steaks
4 tablespoons soy sauce
150 ml (¼ pint) fish or vegetable stock
salt and freshly ground black pepper
coriander sprigs, to garnish

1 Dry-fry the onion in a non-stick frying-pan for 2 minutes. Add the lemon grass and ginger, stir well, then add the mushrooms, red pepper and Thai seasoning. Stir and cook over a low heat for 1 minute.
2 Remove the frying-pan from the heat. Stir in the tomato purée and chopped coriander. Leave to cool. This mixture forms the salmon 'stuffing'.
3 Slice the salmon steaks in half, horizontally. Spread a quarter of the stuffing mix evenly over the base of each steak, then cover with the top layer of the salmon. (If freezing, do so at this point).
4 Preheat the oven to Gas Mark 4/ 180°C/350°F.
5 Arrange the steaks in a baking dish, so that they fit comfortably. Pour over the soy sauce and stock, and season with a little salt and black pepper. Cover with a lid or a piece of foil and bake for 25 minutes.
6 Serve, garnished with sprigs of fresh coriander.

TOP TIP You can only freeze the salmon if it has not been previously frozen so be sure to check with your fishmonger.

VARIATION You can also use 2 teaspoons of the prepared fresh lemon grass and ginger which are now available in small jars.

SPINACH AND SWEET POTATO STEW

POINTS

per recipe: 7   per serving: 1½

V *Serves 4*
Preparation time: 10 minutes
Cooking time: 40 minutes
Calories per serving: 170
Freezing: not recommended

Member Liz Bourne has been a guest house proprietor in the seaside town of Bournemouth in Dorset for several years, so she knows a thing or two about cooking! Lately she has been getting into shape and her recipe for this delicious vegetarian stew has helped her to succeed.

low-fat cooking spray
1 large onion, chopped
2 garlic cloves, crushed
2 tablespoons tomato purée
1 medium sweet potato, peeled and diced
400 g can of tomatoes
400 g can of chick-peas, drained
1 vegetable stock cube
1 large bag of young spinach leaves, washed
salt and freshly ground black pepper

1 Spray a large saucepan 3–4 times with the low-fat cooking spray and heat for a few moments. Add the onion and garlic and cook, stirring, for 4–5 minutes. Add the tomato purée and stir well.
2 Add the sweet potato, tomatoes, chick-peas and stock cube to the saucepan. Bring up to the boil, then reduce the heat and simmer gently, covered, for 30 minutes until the sweet potato is tender.
3 Add the spinach leaves to the saucepan and cook gently for 3–4 minutes, until the leaves have wilted. Stir thoroughly, season to taste, then serve.

TOP TIP For a more substantial meal, serve the stew with a medium portion (4 tablespoons) of boiled rice. This will add 3 Points per serving.

VARIATION Instead of chick-peas, use a can of mixed pulses. The Points will remain the same.

Thai Salmon Surprise: This recipe is great with noodles for a total of 6½ Points.

**Greek Stuffed Chicken Breasts:
A fantastic combination
of flavours.**

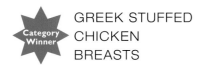

GREEK STUFFED CHICKEN BREASTS

POINTS

per recipe: 9½   per serving: 5

Serves 2
Preparation time: 15 minutes
Cooking time: 20–25 minutes
Calories per serving: 310
Freezing: not recommended

Eileen Walling is a Member who lives in Great Grimsby in North East Lincolnshire. She invented this recipe through her love of chicken and Greek salad, so she combined the two – with great success. The chicken is delicious served with 200 g (7 oz) of boiled new potatoes for each person and fresh watercress. Remember to add 2 Points per serving.

40 g (1½ oz) feta cheese
5 stoned black or green olives, chopped finely
1 teaspoon olive oil
2 medium skinless, boneless chicken breasts
1 aubergine, sliced
2 beefsteak tomatoes, sliced
1 garlic clove, sliced thickly
low-fat cooking spray (preferably olive oil)
salt and freshly ground black pepper

1 Preheat the oven to Gas Mark 6/ 200°C/400°F.
2 Make the stuffing by mashing together the cheese, olives and olive oil with a fork to make a stiff paste.
3 Carefully cut a pocket into the chicken breasts and divide the stuffing mixture between them. Close the pockets and secure with cocktail sticks.
4 Layer the aubergine and tomato slices in a shallow baking dish and slip the slices of garlic between them. Place the stuffed chicken breasts on top, then spray with 2 or 3 squirts of low-fat cooking spray. Season with salt and pepper.
5 Roast for 35–40 minutes until the chicken is cooked. Test with a sharp knife to make sure that the juices run clear.

TOP TIPS If you like, replace the fresh tomatoes with a 400 g can of chopped tomatoes for a runnier sauce.

The stuffing mixture can also be whizzed together in a blender.

SPICY VEGGIE BALLS IN KEFTA SAUCE

POINTS

per recipe: 7   per serving: 1½

 Serves 4
Preparation and cooking time: 1¼ hours
Calories per serving: 190
Freezing: not recommended

Member Flora McLeod lives in Harrogate in North Yorkshire. As a vegetarian, she loves to experiment with recipes to invent something which is not only interesting and tasty but also low in fat and calories to keep the Points low. This really fits the bill. Serve the veggie balls with 4 tablespoons each of rice, remembering to add 3 Points per serving.

1 large red onion, chopped finely
1 vegetable stock cube, dissolved in 150 ml (¼ pint) hot water
225 g (8 oz) Quorn mince
1 tablespoon chopped fresh mint
1 tablespoon chopped fresh parsley
½ teaspoon dried marjoram
75 g (2¾ oz) fresh breadcrumbs
1 egg, beaten
¼ teaspoon ground cumin
¼ teaspoon cayenne pepper
¼ teaspoon paprika
¼ teaspoon mixed spice
salt and freshly ground black pepper

FOR THE SAUCE

3 × 400 g cans of chopped tomatoes
1 red onion, chopped finely
1 tablespoon chopped fresh parsley
1 garlic clove, crushed
300 ml (½ pint) water
a pinch of salt, paprika and cayenne pepper

1 First of all, make the kefta sauce. Put all the sauce ingredients into a large saucepan, heat and simmer gently for 1 hour–1 hour 10 minutes. Meanwhile, make the veggie balls.
2 Preheat the oven to Gas Mark 4/ 180°C/350°F.
3 Put the onion and stock into a saucepan. Heat and simmer for 10 minutes, or until the liquid has just evaporated. Tip into a mixing bowl and allow to cool.
4 Add the Quorn to the onion with all the remaining ingredients. Stir well to combine, then shape into 12 balls.
5 Arrange in a roasting pan or baking dish in a single layer. Roast in the oven for 25–30 minutes, or until browned and crispy on the outside.
6 Put the cooked veggie balls into the sauce and simmer for 5 minutes before serving.

MONDAY'S PIE

POINTS

per recipe: 30   per serving: 7½

Ⓥ *if following variation*
Serves 4
Preparation time: 25 minutes
Cooking time: 20 minutes
Calories per serving: 465
Freezing: recommended

This recipe from Gold Member Rosalind Armstrong from Cramlington in Northumberland is the perfect way to serve leftovers from a roast chicken or turkey. It makes a delicious and filling meal when served with lots of Point-free vegetables.

low-fat cooking spray
125 g (4½ oz) mushrooms, sliced
25 g (1 oz) sauce flour or cornflour
250 ml (9 fl oz) skimmed milk
1 chicken stock cube, dissolved in
150 ml (¼ pint) hot water
225 g (8 oz) cooked chicken, diced
1 tablespoon chopped fresh parsley
1 teaspoon lemon juice
salt and freshly ground black pepper

FOR THE SCONE TOPPING

225 g (8 oz) plain flour
2 teaspoons baking powder
75 g (2¾ oz) polyunsaturated margarine
1 tablespoon chopped fresh parsley

1 Preheat the oven to Gas Mark 7/ 220°C/425°F.

2 Spray a large saucepan 2 or 3 times with low-fat cooking spray. Add the mushrooms and cook them for 3–4 minutes, stirring often.

3 Blend the sauce flour or cornflour with the milk and pour into the saucepan with the stock. Heat gently, stirring constantly, until thickened. Add the chicken, parsley and lemon juice. Season with salt and pepper.

4 Sift the flour and baking powder into a mixing bowl with a pinch of salt. Rub in the margarine using your fingertips, until the mixture resembles fine breadcrumbs. Stir in the parsley, then add sufficient cold water to make a soft, but not sticky, dough.

5 Roll out the dough on a lightly floured surface to a thickness of about 8 mm (⅜-inch).

6 Transfer the chicken mixture to an ovenproof baking dish and top with the pastry crust. Bake for about 20 minutes until browned.

VARIATION Vegetarians can substitute cubed Quorn for the chicken, and use a vegetable stock cube. Points per serving would be 7.

QUORN AU VIN

POINTS

per recipe: 6   per serving: 1½

Ⓥ *Serves 4*
Preparation and cooking time:
45 minutes
Calories per serving: 120
Freezing: recommended

Michele Roberts from Birmingham has been creating lots of new and interesting healthy meals since she has been a Member. Her experience as a chef has helped her, and her family has been the one to benefit – until now, when we can share one of her tasty vegetarian specialities. Serve with lightly cooked vegetables, such as broccoli, carrots and green beans, and 200 g (7 oz) boiled new potatoes, remembering to add 2 Points.

low-fat cooking spray
2 onions, chopped
1 garlic clove, crushed
200 g (7 oz) diced Quorn
200 g (7 oz) mushrooms, sliced
1 vegetable stock cube, dissolved in
350 ml (12 fl oz) hot water
200 ml (7 fl oz) red wine
1 tablespoon tomato purée
1 teaspoon dried mixed herbs
1 tablespoon cornflour
2 tablespoons chopped fresh parsley
salt and freshly ground black pepper

1 Use the low-fat cooking spray to mist the base of a large saucepan. Heat for a few moments, then sauté the onions and garlic until golden, about 5–6 minutes.

2 Add the Quorn and mushrooms and cook, stirring, for 2–3 more minutes. Add the stock and wine, then bring to the boil. Reduce the heat and simmer until the liquid has reduced by approximately one-third.

3 Stir in the tomato purée and herbs. Season to taste, then simmer for 10–15 minutes more.

4 Blend the cornflour with a little cold water and add to the saucepan, stirring until thickened. Add the chopped parsley, then serve.

TOP TIP Prepare the dish the day before to allow the flavours to mellow and intensify. Re-heat thoroughly in the oven or microwave.

TEMPTING THAI TURKEY

POINTS

per recipe: 27½	per serving: 7

Serves 4
Preparation time: 15 minutes
Cooking time: 15 minutes
Calories per serving: 305
Freezing: not recommended

Janet Carney is a Leader from Freckleton, near Preston in Lancashire. Jane loves pure points™ and runs seven Meetings a week to help others to reach their Goal. This recipe is delicious and will help anyone on their way to success.

125 g (4½ oz) Thai stir-fry rice noodles
low-fat cooking spray
450 g (1 lb) turkey steaks, cut into strips
100 g (3½ oz) button mushrooms
2 carrots, cut into matchstick strips
2 onions, sliced
1 green pepper, de-seeded and sliced
1 red pepper, de-seeded and sliced
100 ml (3½ oz) oyster sauce
salt and freshly ground black pepper

1 Soak the rice noodles, according to the pack instructions.
2 Heat a wok or large frying-pan and spray with the low-fat cooking spray. Add the turkey strips and stir-fry over a high heat for 3–4 minutes, until browned. Remove and set aside.
3 Halve the mushrooms and then add all the vegetables to the wok or frying-pan and stir-fry for 4–5 minutes. Add the cooked turkey and oyster sauce, then the drained, soaked noodles.
4 Cook over a low heat, stirring occasionally, until the noodles are heated through. Season to taste, then serve.

VARIATIONS Use any vegetables you like, such as broccoli, courgettes, spring onions and cauliflower – all are Point-free.

Use chicken instead of turkey (Points remain the same).

STICKY PORK

POINTS

per recipe: 8	per serving: 4

Serves 2
Preparation time: 10 minutes + 15–20 minutes to marinate
Cooking time: 10–15 minutes
Calories per serving: 360
Freezing: not recommended

Julie Smith, a Member from Stafford, discovered this delicious pork recipe by accident when she was trying to create a lower-Point version of sweet and sour. It's healthy and tasty – and her partner loves it too.

150 g (5½ oz) lean pork
1 tablespoon clear honey
2 tablespoons sweet chilli sauce
1 tablespoon tomato purée
1 tablespoon Worcestershire sauce
1 teaspoon ground coriander
1 tablespoon chopped fresh coriander
1 tablespoon orange juice
1 garlic clove, crushed

2 teaspoons vegetable oil
1 large onion, sliced
1 red pepper, de-seeded and sliced
1 yellow pepper, de-seeded and sliced
1 large carrot, sliced
6 mushrooms, sliced
40 g (1½ oz) uncooked egg noodles
salt and freshly ground black pepper

1 Put the pork, honey, sweet chilli sauce, tomato purée, Worcestershire sauce, ground and fresh coriander, orange juice and garlic into a bowl. Season with salt and pepper and mix thoroughly. Cover and allow to marinate for about 15–20 minutes.
2 Heat the oil in a wok or large frying-pan over a medium-high heat. Add the onion, pork and marinade. Cook for about 5 minutes, then add the red and yellow peppers, carrot and mushrooms.
3 Continue to cook over a medium-low heat until the pork is glazed and 'sticky', about 8–10 minutes, stirring often.
4 Meanwhile, prepare the noodles according to pack instructions. Serve hot with the sticky pork.

VARIATIONS For a fruity version, add a couple of chopped pineapple rings in natural juice. Drain the juice from the pineapples and use instead of the orange juice (4 Points per serving).

Use cooked rice instead of noodles, if you prefer (3 Points per serving).

Sticky Pork: A very tasty Chinese meal indeed for only 4 Points.

125 g (4½ oz) fine green beans, chopped

2 large carrots, grated

100 g (3½ oz) ready-to-eat dried apricots, chopped

1 tablespoon chopped fresh coriander

salt and freshly ground black pepper

1 Heat the olive oil in a large saucepan, then add the onions. Cover and cook over a low heat for about 5 minutes to sweat them, then add the cumin, turmeric and cinnamon. Cook gently for about 1 minute, being careful not to burn the spices.

2 Add the chicken to the saucepan and cook for about 2 minutes, stirring often, to seal.

3 Pour the stock into the saucepan and add the drained, soaked bulgar wheat. Bring up to the boil, then reduce the heat and simmer until the liquid has reduced.

4 When the liquid has been almost fully absorbed, add the green beans and cook for a few more minutes. Stir in the carrots, apricots and chopped coriander. Heat for a few moments, then season to taste and serve in four warmed bowls.

TOP TIP Add more green vegetables when you're really hungry, without adding further Points. Courgettes or broccoli would be ideal.

VARIATION For a low-Point vegetarian version, omit the chicken and make sure that you use vegetable stock cubes (2 Points per serving.)

Sweet Spices of India: This generous portion is full of the fragrant and enlivening flavours of the East.

SWEET SPICES OF INDIA

POINTS	
per recipe: 16	per serving: 4

Ⓥ *if following variation*

Serves 4

Preparation time: 10 minutes + 1 hour soaking

Cooking time: 20 minutes

Calories per serving: 325

Freezing: recommended

Member Suzanne Jansen from Croydon in Surrey loves to cook which is a good thing since she works in the catering industry! She likes to create new dishes, and admits that she rarely follows a recipe. But we certainly like to follow hers! This one is delicious.

1 teaspoon olive oil
2 onions, chopped
1 teaspoon cumin
1 teaspoon turmeric
1 teaspoon cinnamon
3 medium skinless, boneless chicken breasts, chopped
2 chicken or vegetable stock cubes, dissolved in 400 ml (14 fl oz) hot water
100 g (3½ oz) bulgar wheat, soaked for about 1 hour

ONE POT CHICKEN

POINTS

per recipe: 14   per serving: 3½

Serves 4
Preparation time: 20 minutes
Cooking time: 50 minutes
Calories per serving: 315
Freezing: recommended

Geraldine Parker is a Member from Northampton. She developed this wonderful one-pot chicken dish after a trip to Spain, where she discovered artichoke hearts, and wanted to include them in a few home-cooked recipes – to great effect.

1 tablespoon olive oil

4 medium skinless, boneless chicken breasts

12 shallots, peeled

3 carrots, chopped

2 leeks, sliced

1 tablespoon plain flour

1 chicken stock cube, dissolved in 425 ml (¾ pint) hot water

100 ml (3½ fl oz) skimmed milk

4 canned artichokes, drained and halved

2 red peppers, de-seeded and chopped into thick strips

1 tablespoon wholegrain mustard

salt and freshly ground black pepper

1 Preheat the oven to Gas Mark 3/ 170°C/325°F.

2 Heat half the olive oil in a non-stick frying-pan, add the chicken breasts and cook over a high heat for 1 minute, or until golden. Turn them over and cook for another minute or so. Transfer the chicken to an ovenproof casserole dish.

3 Add the shallots to the frying-pan and stir-fry them for 1–2 minutes, or until light golden brown, then transfer them to the casserole. Add the carrots and leeks to the casserole dish.

4 Heat the remaining oil in the frying-pan and add the flour, stirring with a wooden spoon. Cook over a medium heat for 1 minute, stirring, then gradually add the stock, stirring as you go. When all the stock has been incorporated, stir in the milk and season.

5 Pour the sauce over the chicken. Cover with a lid or a piece of foil and transfer to the oven to cook for 30 minutes.

6 Add the artichokes and red peppers. Cook for a further 15 minutes, or until the vegetables are tender. Just before serving, stir in the wholegrain mustard.

TOP TIP Serve with spinach or green beans for no extra Points, and boiled new potatoes (200 g/7 oz per person), adding 2 Points each.

VARIATION Add a chopped red or green fresh chilli if you like a bit of heat.

One Pot Chicken: Why not serve this Spanish dish in the rustic style and take the whole dish to the table, as pictured here?

CHICKEN AND BANANA WRAPS

POINTS

per recipe: 17   per serving: 4

Serves 4
Preparation time: 10 minutes
Cooking time: 25–30 minutes
Calories per serving: 310
Freezing: not recommended

Mary Stickland from Solihull in the West Midlands has been a Member for over 20 years – her weekly Meeting keeping her on track – and she's now a Gold Member. Her recipe for chicken-wrapped bananas is delicious, and it's perfect for entertaining.

4 medium skinless, boneless chicken breasts
4 small bananas
8 × 98% fat-free turkey rashers
low-fat cooking spray
salt and freshly ground black pepper

1 Preheat the oven to Gas Mark 4/ 180°C/350°F.
2 Using a rolling pin, flatten out the chicken breasts until thin. Do this between pieces of clingfilm, if you like.
3 Place a peeled banana on top of each flattened chicken breast, then roll up. Wrap two turkey rashers around each one, and secure with cocktail sticks.
4 Spray four large squares of foil with low-fat cooking spray and place a wrapped chicken piece on top of each one. Season with a little salt and pepper. Wrap the foil around the chicken to form a loose parcel.
5 Place the parcels on a baking tray and cook in the oven for 30–40 minutes, or until the chicken is done. To test that it is ready, pierce the chicken with a sharp knife or skewer; the juices should run clear. If not, return to the oven for a few more minutes.

VARIATION Use ready-to-eat dried apricots instead of the bananas. Use three per chicken breast. The Points per serving will be 3½.

Salmon and Asparagus Supreme: The perfect combination of ingredients for spring or summer.

SALMON AND ASPARAGUS SUPREME

POINTS

per recipe: 9½   per serving: 5

Serves 2
Preparation time: 10 minutes
Cooking time: 40 minutes
Calories per serving: 310
Freezing: recommended

Mrs D. Hargate from Keelby in Lincolnshire is a keen walker, a keen cook and a Gold Member! She has dreamt up a fabulous fish dish.

2 large leeks, sliced
2 large courgettes, sliced
6 large asparagus spears, trimmed
125 g (4½ oz) smoked salmon
2 teaspoons low-fat spread
1 tablespoon cornflour
300 ml (½ pint) skimmed milk
2 tablespoons grated parmesan cheese
salt and freshly ground black pepper

1 Preheat the oven to Gas Mark 5/ 190°C/375°F.
2 Cook the leeks and courgettes for about 4–5 minutes in lightly salted boiling water, until just tender. Meanwhile, cook the asparagus in a separate saucepan for the same length of time. Drain and leave to cool.
3 Wrap pieces of smoked salmon around the asparagus spears.
4 Layer half the quantity of courgettes and leeks in an ovenproof baking dish. Season with salt and pepper. Lay the wrapped asparagus spears on top, then finish with the remaining courgettes and leeks. Season lightly.
5 Put the low-fat spread, cornflour, milk and parmesan cheese into a saucepan. Heat, stirring constantly with a small whisk, until thickened and smooth. Season, then pour over the vegetables in the baking dish.
6 Bake for approximately 25–30 minutes, until piping hot.

**Steak Fajitas:
Two fajitas for
only 3½ Points!**

STEAK FAJITAS

POINTS

per recipe: 14	per serving: 3½

Serves 4

Preparation time: 10 minutes + 1 hour marinating

Cooking time: 10 minutes

Calories per serving: 385

Freezing: not recommended

Anita Mulholland is a Member from Birmingham. She developed this recipe as a quick and easy way to introduce more fresh food into her diet since her busy lifestyle allows little time for cooking. Serve with a green leafy salad.

175 g (6 oz) lean braising steak, cut into strips

juice of 1 lime

1–2 garlic cloves, crushed

2 teaspoons olive oil

8 small soft flour tortillas

1 green pepper, de-seeded and cut into strips

1 red pepper, de-seeded and cut into strips

125 g (4½ oz) mushrooms, sliced

1 onion, sliced

2 tomatoes, sliced

salt and freshly ground black pepper

green leafy salad, to serve

1 Put the steak into a bowl with the lime juice, garlic and 1 teaspoon of olive oil. Cover and refrigerate for about 1 hour.

2 Preheat the oven to Gas Mark 4/ 180°C/350°F.

3 Wrap the tortillas in foil and warm them in the oven for about 10 minutes.

4 Meanwhile, heat a wok or large frying-pan and add the remaining oil. Stir-fry the marinated steak for 2 minutes, then add all the vegetables and stir-fry for a further 4–5 minutes. Season with salt and pepper.

5 Divide the stir-fry between the warmed tortillas, then roll up and serve two fajitas per person with the green salad.

VARIATION Use turkey or chicken stir-fry strips instead of steak. The Points per serving would be 3.

GAMMON IN RAISIN SAUCE

POINTS

per recipe: 17	per serving: 4

Serves 4

Preparation time: 10 minutes

Cooking time: 25-30 minutes

Calories per serving: 260

Freezing: not recommended

Member Anne Brown from Camberley in Surrey has cooked this tasty gammon recipe many times; it's a real family favourite. Although raisin sauce sounds a bit unusual – rest assured, it is absolutely delicious!

500 g (1 lb 2 oz) smoked gammon steaks, about 1 cm (½-inch) thick

low-fat cooking spray

1 onion, chopped finely

2 tablespoons raisins

8 thin strips of orange peel

300 ml (½ pint) dry cider

1 tablespoon cornflour

150 ml (¼ pint) fresh orange juice

freshly ground black pepper

1 Cut each gammon slice into four equal pieces and remove the rind and the fat.

2 Spray a large heavy-based frying-pan with the low-fat cooking spray and heat for a few moments. Add the gammon pieces, searing them on both sides.

3 Add the onion, raisins, orange peel and cider. Heat, then cover and simmer for 25–30 minutes.

4 Blend the cornflour into the orange juice. Lift the gammon from the frying-pan and keep warm. Stir the orange juice mixture into the frying-pan and heat until thickened. Bubble for a few moments, then season with pepper and serve with the gammon.

VARIATION You could use unsweetened apple juice instead of cider. The Points will remain the same.

Gammon in Raisin Sauce: The sweet raisin sauce makes the gammon incredibly tasty.

Strawberry and
Apple Filo Tart:
The perfect way
to finish a meal
and no one will
guess that you
are dieting! It's
only 2½ Points
per serving.

desserts

Now here is a section that most Weight Watchers Members know something about! Desserts are so often a dieter's downfall. You know the score – first you deprive yourself by refusing even the smallest slice, then the willpower fails and you eat heaps instead.

With the flexibility of **pure points**™ and these recipes, things will be different. You'll be able to eat and enjoy your share of the goodies without feeling the slightest twinge of guilt. The recipes are low in Points – but the best thing is, they taste utterly fantastic. Many thanks to all who sent in these delicious desserts – for looking after our waistlines.

STRAWBERRY AND APPLE FILO TART

POINTS

per recipe: 13½   per serving: 2½

Ⓥ Serves 6
Preparation time: 20 minutes
Cooking time: 30 minutes
Calories per serving: 155
Freezing: not recommended

Member Alison Winter is a surgeon from Glasgow. She keeps her sweet tooth in check by creating delicious recipes like this one. It's perfect for dinner parties since dieters can eat it without feeling guilty.

low-fat cooking spray
150 g (5½ oz) filo pastry
3 medium eating apples
50 ml (2 fl oz) fresh orange juice
2 tablespoons granulated sweetener
300 g (10½ oz) strawberries, hulled and halved

TO SERVE
2 teaspoons icing sugar
6 tablespoons half-fat crème fraîche

1 Preheat the oven to Gas Mark 6/ 200°C/400°F. Spray the base of a 23 cm (9-inch) flan tin with low-fat cooking spray.

2 Line the flan tin with half the pastry sheets, spraying each sheet with low-fat cooking spray and overlapping the edges of the tin slightly.

3 Bake for 10 minutes in the centre of the oven.

4 Meanwhile, peel, core and slice the apples, then put them in a saucepan with the orange juice. Cover and simmer for about 5–8 minutes, until tender. Remove from the heat and add the granulated sweetener and strawberries, mixing gently. Use to fill the cooked flan case.

5 Tear the remaining pastry sheets into strips and arrange them loosely over the tart. Spray two or three times with low-fat cooking spray, then bake for a further 15–20 minutes.

6 Cool the tart for a few minutes, then serve, dusted with icing sugar and accompanied by the crème fraîche.

TOP TIP Use sunflower low-fat cooking spray instead of the olive oil variety; its flavour is more suitable.

VARIATION Try using peaches and apricots when they are in season – either alone or together.

CHOCOLATE MOUSSE

POINTS

per recipe: 16	per serving: 2½

 Serves 6
Preparation time: 15 minutes + chilling
Calories per serving: 105
Freezing: not recommended

This is such an incredibly easy recipe for chocolate mousse from Gold Member Valerie Gough who lives in Havant, Hampshire. It satisfies the desire for chocolate, without piling up the Points and it's perfect for a special dessert.

100 g (3½ oz) good quality dark chocolate (70% cocoa solids)
3 egg whites
175 g (6 oz) raspberries

TO DECORATE
mint leaves
1 teaspoon icing sugar

1 Break the chocolate into pieces and put them in a large heatproof bowl.
2 Position the bowl over a saucepan of gently simmering water and melt the chocolate. Be careful that you don't allow any water to get into the bowl. Remove the melted chocolate from the heat and allow to cool slightly.
3 In a large grease-free bowl, and using scrupulously clean beaters, whisk the egg whites until stiff.

4 Using a large metal spoon, fold one tablespoon of the egg white through the chocolate to 'loosen' it, then fold in the remaining egg white, taking care that you do this gently, so you don't lose too much air as the volume will decrease.
5 Divide the mixture between six small serving glasses or dishes, allowing enough space to finish off with the raspberries. Refrigerate until set.
6 Serve, topped with the raspberries, and decorated with mint leaves and a dusting of icing sugar.

VARIATION Try using ginger-flavoured chocolate, and decorate with finely sliced stem ginger instead of raspberries and mint leaves.

SUSAN'S ZABAGLIONE

POINTS

per recipe: 9½	per serving: 2½

Serves 4
Preparation and cooking time: 25 minutes + chilling
Calories per serving: 105
Freezing: not recommended

Since losing weight and becoming a Leader in Easingwold, Thirsk and Bedale in North Yorkshire, Susan Anderson has radically changed her eating habits – and those of her family. Now they all enjoy a much healthier diet. This Italian-inspired dessert helps her to stay at Goal Weight.

1 sachet of lemon pie filling
1 egg, separated
25 g (1 oz) caster sugar
100 ml (3½ fl oz) white wine
100 g carton low-fat plain fromage frais
a few drops of lemon juice
artificial sweetener, to taste (optional)
1 square of chocolate, grated

1 Empty the sachet of lemon pie filling into a saucepan and blend in 250 ml (9 fl oz) cold water and the egg yolk. Cook gently, stirring constantly, until the mixture boils and thickens, checking that the flavour capsule dissolves if there is one. Remove from the heat and allow to cool for a few minutes.
2 Whisk the egg white in a grease-free bowl until stiff peaks form.

Whisk in the caster sugar. Add the wine and the slightly cooled lemon mixture, folding in gently to combine. Divide between four serving glasses and cool completely, then cover and chill in the refrigerator.
3 Just before serving, flavour the fromage frais with a little lemon juice and artificial sweetener (if desired) and use to top the desserts. Finish off with the grated chocolate.

TOP TIP Remember that egg white will not whisk successfully if there is the slightest trace of grease or egg yolk in the bowl or on the beaters. It's always a good precaution to wash the bowl and beaters in hot soapy water before you begin.

**Chocolate Mousse:
A Weight Watchers
miracle at only 2½
Points per serving!**

Red Cherry and Ginger Slice: Not only is this a wonderful dessert to eat, it's so pretty to serve and is a mere 3½ Points per serving.

RED CHERRY AND GINGER SLICE

POINTS

per recipe: 29½	per serving: 3½

Serves 8
Preparation time: 25 minutes +
several hours chilling
Calories per serving: 200
Freezing: not recommended

Member Janet Smith from Scarborough in North Yorkshire has devised this indulgent dessert to keep sweet cravings at bay. It uses low-fat ingredients to keep the Points in check, though you'd never guess it was a Weight Watchers pudding.

50 g (1¾ oz) polyunsaturated margarine
150 g (5½ oz) Rich Tea or Morning Coffee biscuits
½ teaspoon ground ginger
4 tablespoons boiling water
12 g sachet of powdered gelatine
397 g can of cherry pie filling
4 teaspoons artificial sweetener
500 g carton virtually fat-free fromage frais
25 g (1 oz) crystallised ginger

1 Line an 18 cm (7-inch) loose-based cake tin with clingfilm.
2 Melt the margarine and stir in the crushed biscuits and ground ginger. Tip them into the prepared tin and press down evenly over the base. Chill in the refrigerator.
3 Put 4 tablespoons of just-boiled water into a bowl and sprinkle in the gelatine. Stir to disperse, then allow 4–5 minutes for it to dissolve into a completely clear liquid.

4 Tip the cherry pie filling into a mixing bowl and add the gelatine liquid, stirring thoroughly. Add the sweetener, then fold in the fromage frais. Pour this mixture over the biscuit base and spread out evenly. Cover and chill for several hours, or overnight, to set.
5 Just before serving, carefully lift from the tin and remove the clingfilm. Cut into eight portions and decorate with finely chopped crystallised ginger.

VARIATIONS Try a different pie filling, such as blackcurrant or raspberry.

Use stem ginger in syrup, well-rinsed, instead of the crystallised ginger.

QUICK BAKED APPLES WITH PLUMS AND SULTANAS

POINTS

per recipe: 11	per serving: 2½

 Serves 4
Preparation time: 15 minutes
Cooking time: 6–8 minutes
Calories per serving: 130
Freezing: not recommended

Ann Stewart is a Member and a busy mother of three from Liverpool. She loves her Meetings – finding them friendly, helpful, supportive and fun! This easy dessert satisfies her sweet tooth, without piling up the Points.

4 medium cooking apples, peeled and cored
6 plums, stoned and sliced
1 heaped tablespoon sultanas
artificial sweetener, to taste
4 heaped tablespoons reduced-sugar strawberry jam

1 Put the cooking apples in a microwaveable dish. Mix the plums with the sultanas and use this mixture to fill the cavities in the apples.
2 Sprinkle the apples with artificial sweetener, then place a heaped tablespoon of strawberry jam on top of each one.
3 Cook in the microwave on HIGH for 6–8 minutes, or until the apples are tender and the jam has melted. Or cook in the oven at Gas Mark 4/180°C/350°F for 40 minutes.
4 Serve the apples with the hot syrupy mixture spooned over and around them.

VARIATION For a real treat, serve the apples with 2 small (150 g) pots of low-fat custard to add 1 extra Point per serving.

Quick Baked Apples: Incredibly satisfying.

CITRUS CHOCOLATE SPICE PUDDING

POINTS

per recipe: 11   per serving: 2½

Ⓥ *if using free-range eggs*
Serves 4
Preparation and cooking time:
20 minutes
Calories per serving: 175
Freezing: not recommended

Jill Mack is a Member from Sutton-in-Trent in Nottinghamshire. She has invented this quick and easy low-Point light sponge pudding to cook in the microwave. If you've never cooked a sponge like this before, you're in for a treat, as it literally rises in front of your eyes.

low-fat cooking spray
100 g (3½ oz) grapefruit segments
½ teaspoon ground ginger (optional)
4 heaped teaspoons low-calorie marmalade
50 g (1¾ oz) caster sugar
2 medium eggs
50 g (1¾ oz) self-raising flour
15 g (½ oz) cocoa powder

1 Spray a 1.2 litre (2 pint) pudding basin with low-fat cooking spray.
2 Put the grapefruit segments into the basin. Mix the ginger, if using, and 2 teaspoons of water into the marmalade, then spoon this mixture over the grapefruit.
3 Using a hand-held electric mixer, whisk the sugar and eggs together until very light and thick; this will take about 5 minutes.
4 Sift the flour and cocoa powder together, the gently fold into the whisked mixture, using a large metal spoon to retain as much air as possible. Transfer this mixture to the pudding basin.
5 To cook in the microwave, cover the basin with microwave-safe clingfilm and pierce it 2 or 3 times. Cook in the microwave on HIGH for 2½–3 minutes, or until risen and spongy. Allow to stand for 3 minutes before serving. To cook in a steamer, cover the pudding with foil or greaseproof paper and steam for 1 hour 10 minutes, making sure that the steamer does not boil dry.

VARIATION Use a peeled and segmented orange – with all the pith removed – instead of the grapefruit segments. The Points will remain the same.

STRAWBERRY CLOUD

POINTS

per recipe: 8   per serving: 1½

Ⓥ *if using a free-range egg*
Serves 6
Preparation time: 25 minutes + chilling
Calories per serving: 95
Freezing: not recommended

Gold Member Linda Sutherland from Saline in Fife, Scotland, has sent in this very easy light-as-air dessert. It's perfect if, like her, you grow your own strawberries, though it makes a few go a long way.

225 g (8 oz) strawberries, hulled
1 egg white
75 g (2¾ oz) icing sugar
1 tablespoon lemon juice
6 After Eight mints, cut in half to form triangles

1 Wash the strawberries and pat dry thoroughly with kitchen paper. Put them into a bowl and mash with a fork or potato masher.
2 Beat the egg white in a grease-free bowl using a hand-held electric whisk until stiff peaks form, then gradually whisk in the icing sugar.
3 Gradually whisk in the strawberries, then whisk on high speed for 4–5 minutes until the mixture is light, foamy and thick. Whisk in the lemon juice, then spoon into six individual dishes.
4 Cover and chill in the refrigerator until ready to serve. Decorate each one with an After Eight mint.

TOP TIP You can make this dessert in advance, allowing it to chill in the refrigerator overnight.

VARIATIONS Make up a strawberry or lemon-flavoured sugar-free jelly and set in the bottom of six tall serving glasses, then top with Strawberry Cloud for no extra Points.

Instead of the mints, sprinkle each dessert with a tiny amount of cocoa powder. This will reduce the Points to 1 per serving.

Citrus Chocolate
Spice Pudding:
Light, chocolatey
and spicy and
only 2½ Points
per serving.

Roly Pavlova:
Each delicious
slice is only
3 Points.

ROLY PAVLOVA

POINTS

per recipe: 24   per serving: 3

ⓥ if using free-range eggs
Serves 8
Preparation time: 10 minutes +
cooling time
Cooking time: 45 minutes
Calories per serving: 170
Freezing: not recommended

Jill Seaman is a Gold Member from
Bognor Regis in West Sussex. As a
food technology teacher she is eager
to promote healthy eating to her
pupils and her family! Her recipe
for fruit-filled meringue is low in fat,
and because it is gluten-free, it's also
suitable for coeliacs.

1 teaspoon vanilla essence
1 teaspoon vinegar
1 teaspoon cornflour
4 medium egg whites
200 g (7 oz) caster sugar
200 ml (7 fl oz) half-fat crème fraîche
500 g (1 lb 2 oz) frozen summer fruits,
defrosted and drained

1 Preheat the oven to Gas Mark 2/
150°C/300°F. Line a 23 × 33 cm
(9 × 13-inch) Swiss roll tin with
baking parchment.
2 Blend together the vanilla essence,
vinegar and cornflour.
3 Using a hand-held electric mixer,
whisk the egg whites in a grease-free
bowl until stiff peaks form. Whisk
in the caster sugar and cornflour
mixture in three equal quantities and
continue whisking until the mixture
is thick and glossy.
4 Spoon the meringue into the
prepared tin and level the surface.
Bake in the oven for 45 minutes,
then turn off the oven. Leave the
meringue in the cooling oven for
15 minutes.
5 Turn the meringue out on to a
large sheet of greaseproof paper
and carefully peel off the baking
parchment. Allow to cool completely.
6 Spread the crème fraîche over the
meringue and sprinkle with the fruit.
Gently roll up from the narrow end,
then serve.

TOP TIP Do not worry if the
meringue cracks when you roll
it up; it adds to its charm.

VARIATION When soft summer
fruits are in season, use them instead
of frozen summer berries. Reserve a
few for decoration for a professional
finish.

FRUITY MERINGUE

POINTS

per recipe: 10   per serving: 2¹/₂

ⓥ if using free-range eggs
Serves 4
Preparation and cooking time:
25 minutes
Calories per serving: 140
Freezing: not recommended

Member Teg Morse from Hereford
has done really well on pure points™,
and her husband has lost weight too,
just by eating the same things. She
loves to cook for her family, and
enjoys trying out new low-fat recipes
and inventing some of her own.

100 g (3¹/₂ oz) blackberries
100 g (3¹/₂ oz) blackcurrants or
redcurrants
100 g (3¹/₂ oz) blueberries
150 g (5¹/₂ oz) raspberries
150 g (5¹/₂ oz) strawberries, hulled
50 g (1³/₄ oz) black grapes
artificial sweetener, to taste
3 egg whites
3 tablespoons caster sugar
4 tablespoons single cream

1 Preheat the oven to Gas Mark 4/
180°C/350°F.
2 Prepare all the fruit, cutting any
large strawberries in half. Put them
all into a large baking dish with 2
tablespoons of cold water and bake
for about 5–6 minutes, until the juice
starts to run. Remove from the oven
and sweeten to taste with artificial
sweetener.
3 Whisk the egg whites in a grease-
free bowl until stiff peaks form, then
whisk in the sugar. Pile the meringue
on top of the fruit and bake for about
5–6 minutes until golden brown.
4 Serve whilst warm, with 1
tablespoon of single cream per
portion.

VARIATION If you can't find all
the different types of fruit, make
substitutions. For example, use
cherries instead of blackberries,
or just use more of the varieties
you have.

RHUBARB LASAGNE

POINTS

per recipe: 10   per serving: 2½

 Serves 4
Preparation time: 35 minutes
Cooking time: 30 minutes
Calories per serving: 215
Freezing: not recommended

Glynis Kennedy, a Member from Romford in Essex, has developed this ingenious recipe for a sweet lasagne, using the classic combination of rhubarb and custard with ready-to-cook lasagne sheets. It's delicious!

500 g (1 lb 2 oz) fresh rhubarb, cut into 2.5 cm (1-inch) chunks

2 heaped tablespoons powdered sweetener

125 g (4½ oz) no-need to pre-cook lasagne sheets (6 sheets)

425 g can of low-fat custard

2 teaspoons (10 g) flaked almonds

1 Preheat the oven to Gas Mark 8/ 230°C/450°F.
2 Put the rhubarb into a baking dish, sprinkle with 2 tablespoons of water, then bake for about 5–8 minutes until tender. Remove from the oven and sprinkle with the sweetener.
3 Reduce the oven temperature to Gas Mark 5/190°C/375°F.
4 Spoon half the rhubarb into a 23 × 18 cm (9 × 7-inch) baking dish and top with 2 lasagne sheets. Cover with half the custard, spreading it over evenly. Add another 2 sheets of lasagne, then the remaining rhubarb. Top with the last 2 sheets of lasagne and spread the remaining custard over the surface. Sprinkle with the flaked almonds.
5 Bake in the oven for 25–30 minutes, then serve.

VARIATION When rhubarb is out of season use 2 medium baking apples instead, with 1 heaped tablespoon of raisins or sultanas added. Add 1 Point per serving.

HOT CHOCOLATE CAKE

POINTS

per recipe: 15½   per serving: 4

 if using a free-range egg
Serves 4
Preparation and cooking time: 10 minutes
Calories per serving: 225
Freezing: recommended

Serena Beaumont is a Gold Member from Towcester in Northamptonshire and she devised this delicious recipe to indulge her passion for chocolate and cake. As a mother of two boys, Serena really appreciates the fact that this delicious low-Point chocolate favourite is so easy to make.

55 g (2 oz) polyunsaturated margarine

55 g (2 oz) caster sugar

1 egg

40 g (1½ oz) self-raising flour

15 g (½ oz) cocoa powder

1 Cream together the margarine and sugar in a 1.2 litre (2 pint) pudding basin.
2 Beat in the egg and then carefully fold in the flour and cocoa powder.
3 Mix well and then microwave on HIGH for 2 minutes.
4 Allow to stand for 3–4 minutes, then turn out and serve immediately.

TOP TIPS Step 4 recommends that you eat it immediately because this cake dries out quickly so be sure to have some friends ready and waiting when you bake it!

If you have any Points to spare, serve with half a 150 g pot of hot low-fat custard for 1 Point.

**Rhubarb Lasagne:
An unusual and
delicious dessert
which is sure to
be a talking point!
2½ Points per
serving.**

Eazi-Freeze Lemon Sponge: Bursting with flavour and perfect with a cup of tea. Only 3 Points per slice.

You'll find some truly scrumptious recipes in this chapter of delicious home-bakes. There's something quite therapeutic about home baking – the delicious aromas and sense of satisfaction are hard to beat. And many of the recipes can be frozen so you can just take what you want to eat now and save the rest for another time such as when friends drop in.

EAZI-FREEZE LEMON SPONGE

POINTS

per recipe: 50½   per slice: 3

Ⓥ *if using free-range eggs*

Serves 16
Preparation time: 15 minutes
Cooking time: 1 hour
Calories per slice: 190
Freezing: recommended

Member Megan Thomas lives in Newmarket, Suffolk, where she attends her local Meeting. She devised this recipe as a quick and easy low-fat treat. If you wrap and freeze pieces individually, you'll have the ideal solution for perfect portion control. This is delicious with 2 tablespoons of virtually fat-free fromage frais. The Points will remain the same.

low-fat cooking spray
juice and finely grated zest of 1 lemon
150 g (5½ oz) caster sugar
150 ml carton of low-fat plain yogurt
150 ml (5 fl oz) sunflower oil
250 g (9 oz) self-raising flour
2 large eggs

1 Preheat the oven to Gas Mark 3/ 170°C/325°F. Spray a 20 cm (8-inch) round cake tin with low-fat cooking spray and line with greaseproof paper.
2 Put the lemon juice into a bowl and add one teaspoon of the caster sugar.
3 Put the lemon zest into a large mixing bowl and add the remaining sugar, yogurt, oil, flour and eggs. Beat together for 1 minute with a wooden spoon to mix thoroughly.
4 Pour the mixture into the prepared tin, then transfer to the middle shelf of the oven and bake for approximately 1 hour or until risen and springy when lightly touched.

5 Stand the cake tin on a cooling rack, and while hot, slowly spoon the lemon juice mixture over the cake. Allow to cool in the tin.
6 When completely cooled, cut the cake into 16 portions.

TOP TIPS Wrap the portions not required in freezer wrap, then freeze for up to 2 months. Only defrost portions required, to reduce temptation!

Use the empty yogurt carton as an easy measure to make the cake even quicker to prepare. You'll need 2 × caster sugar, 1 × sunflower oil and 3 × self-raising flour. Points remain the same.

VARIATION Try using orange zest and juice for a change.

BETTER BROWNIES

POINTS

per recipe: 26½   per brownie: 2

Ⓥ if using free-range eggs

Makes 12

Preparation time: 15 minutes +
15 minutes cooling

Cooking time: 25 minutes

Calories per brownie: 135

Freezing: recommended

Member Elena Graham from Kilmarnock in Ayrshire has lived in Canada most of her life and it's there that she acquired a love for chocolate brownies. For a decadent treat, serve with a scoop of Weight Watchers from Heinz Vanilla Flavour Iced Dessert and add 1½ Points per serving.

low-fat cooking spray

75 g (2¾ oz) self-raising flour

50 g (1¾ oz) unsweetened cocoa powder

¼ teaspoon salt

1 large egg

2 egg whites

175 g (6 oz) caster sugar

6 tablespoons unsweetened apple sauce

2 tablespoons sunflower oil

2 teaspoons vanilla essence

15 g (½ oz) chopped walnuts

1 Preheat the oven to Gas Mark 4/ 180°C/350°F. Spray a 20 cm (8-inch) square non-stick baking pan with the low-fat cooking spray.

2 In a medium bowl, combine the flour, cocoa powder and salt, stirring together to mix.

3 In a large mixing bowl, whisk together the egg, egg whites, sugar, apple sauce, oil and vanilla.

4 Add the flour mixture to the egg mixture, stirring until just blended. Take care not to over-mix, or else the brownies will not rise.

5 Transfer the cake mixture to the baking pan and sprinkle with the walnuts.

6 Bake in the centre of the oven until just set – about 25 minutes. A toothpick or skewer inserted in the centre of the cake should come out clean.

7 Cool in the tin for 15 minutes, then cut into 12 rectangles.

TOP TIP If you don't have a non-stick cake pan, it is advisable to line your tin with greaseproof paper.

VARIATION Use chopped pecans or almonds instead of walnuts, if you prefer. The Points will remain the same.

**Carrot Bread:
Each delicious
slice is only
1 Point.**

CARROT BREAD

POINTS

per recipe: 25   per slice: 1

Ⓥ if using a free-range egg

Serves 24

Preparation time: 10 minutes

Cooking time: 25 minutes +
standing time

Calories per slice: 70

Freezing: recommended

Gold Member Jaki Crook from Clitheroe in Lancashire has set her sights on becoming a Leader. She created this quick carrot bread which is cooked in the microwave. It's filling and tasty, yet low in Points.

175 g (6 oz) self-raising flour

50 g (1¾ oz) caster sugar

2 teaspoons baking powder

1 teaspoon mixed spice

1 teaspoon salt

1 teaspoon vanilla essence

1 egg

2 tablespoons olive oil

100 ml (3½ fl oz) skimmed milk

175 g (6 oz) raisins

300 g (10½ oz) grated carrots

1 Put all the ingredients into a large mixing bowl, adding the raisins and carrots last of all. Mix together.

2 Divide the mixture between two oval Pyrex dishes, about 20 cm (8 inches) in length.

3 Microwave each one separately for 12 minutes on HIGH, allowing them to stand for at least 5 minutes.

4 Turn out onto a wire rack, then cool before cutting.

TOP TIP To bake in the oven, use two 450 g (1 lb) loaf tins. Grease with low-fat cooking spray. Line with greaseproof paper. Bake for about 45–50 minutes at Gas Mark 6/ 200°C/400°F or until a skewer comes out clean.

Banana and
Sultana Loaf:
Time to put on
the coffee pot!
Only 2 Points
per slice.

BANANA AND SULTANA LOAF

POINTS

per recipe: 35½   per slice: 2

V if using free-range eggs

Serves 16

Preparation time: 10 minutes + cooling

Cooking time: 1 hour–1 hour
10 minutes

Calories per slice: 150

Freezing: recommended

Member Mary Littlefair from Ashbourne in Derbyshire has really done well with her quest to lose weight, thanks to Weight Watchers. She has developed this scrumptious cake and finds it fits in well with *pure points*™.

---

low-fat cooking spray

5 medium bananas, peeled

2 medium eggs, beaten

175 g (6 oz) soft brown sugar

100 g (3½ oz) sultanas

225 g (8 oz) wholemeal self-raising flour

---

1 Preheat the oven to Gas Mark 4/ 180°C/350°F. Grease a 1 kg (2 lb 4 oz) loaf tin with low-fat cooking spray and line with greaseproof paper.

2 Mash the bananas in a large mixing bowl and add the eggs, sugar and sultanas. Stir in the flour.

3 Transfer the mixture to the prepared tin and level the surface. Bake for 1 hour–1 hour 10 minutes, covering with foil half-way through. The loaf is ready when a skewer inserted into the centre of the cake comes out clean.

4 Cool in the tin for 10 minutes, then remove from the tin and cool on a wire rack.

TOP TIPS The cake is best when kept in an airtight tin for 24 hours before serving.

A potato masher is the ideal utensil for mashing the bananas; otherwise just use a fork.

VARIATION You could also use the same quantity of white self-raising flour. The Points per serving would be the same.

HEALTHY HERB BREAD

POINTS

per recipe: 63   per slice: 2

V Serves 30

Preparation time: 25 minutes + 1 hour 40 minutes rising time

Cooking time: 50 minutes

Calories per slice: 135

Freezing: recommended

Ragnhild Myklebust is a Member from Norway who now lives in Walton-on-Thames in Surrey. She loves to cook and enjoys baking bread and making home-made jam and pickles, though recently she has turned her skills into making wooden toys and decorations – a very talented lady!

---

500 g (1 lb 2 oz) strong white bread flour

300 g (10½ oz) soft grain strong white flour

100 g (3½ oz) coarse wheat bran

50 g (1¾ oz) coarse rye flour

50 g (1¾ oz) coarse oatmeal

100 g (3½ oz) sunflower, pumpkin and linseeds, mixed

1 packet of easy-blend yeast

1 tablespoon salt

15 g (½ oz) fresh mixed herbs (e.g. parsley, thyme, rosemary, marjoram, chives)

250 g (9 oz) low-fat plain yogurt

850 ml (1½ pints) lukewarm water

1 tablespoon olive oil

low-fat cooking spray

---

1 In a very large mixing bowl, combine all the dry ingredients together.

2 In a large jug, mix together the yogurt and lukewarm water. Add to the flour mixture and stir to combine, then transfer to a floured surface and knead for 10–15 minutes until the dough is smooth and elastic.

3 Put the dough into the clean bowl and smear the olive oil on top. Cover the bowl with clingfilm or a clean, damp tea towel and leave for about an hour in a draught-free place, or until the dough has roughly doubled in size.

4 Knock back the dough by punching it with your fist and then knead lightly for a few moments. Divide into two equal pieces and form into two ovals. Place onto separate baking sheets, greased with low-fat cooking spray. Allow to rise in a warm place for a further 30–40 minutes.

5 Preheat the oven to Gas Mark 5/ 190°C/375°F.

6 Bake for 40–50 minutes, or until the loaves are well-risen and golden brown. They should have a hollow sound when tapped lightly on their bases.

TOP TIP Sprinkling the surface of the loaves with a little cold water just before putting them into the oven will help them to rise.

few moments. Add the onion and cook for 2–3 minutes, then add the turkey rashers and cook, stirring, for another 2 minutes. Remove from the heat.

3 Put the flour, salt, paprika and baking powder into a mixing bowl. Stir well. Add the low-fat spread and rub in, using your fingertips, until the mixture resembles fine breadcrumbs.

4 Stir in the cooled onion mixture and half the grated cheese. Mix the egg and milk together, then add to the mixing bowl and stir until just combined.

5 Spoon the mixture into the prepared muffin tins and sprinkle with the remaining cheese.

6 Bake for 20 minutes until risen and golden brown. Cool on a wire rack.

TOP TIP Make sure that you use proper cook's measuring spoons. This is vital when measuring baking powder; level off the surface with a knife for an accurate amount.

VARIATION Add a tablespoon of chopped fresh herbs, such as chives or parsley to the mixture. Or try a teaspoon of mixed dried herbs instead.

Must-Have Muffins: These moist and savoury muffins would be ideal with soup or a light meal.

MUST-HAVE MUFFINS

POINTS

per recipe: 34   **per muffin: 3**

Makes 12
Preparation time: 20 minutes + cooling
Cooking time: 20 minutes
Calories per muffin: 170
Freezing: recommended

Lin Spicer is a Member from Halton in Buckinghamshire who loves to cook. She created this super recipe for a fellow Member who missed eating cheese. These muffins satisfy the craving, without blowing all your Points.

low-fat cooking spray

1 large onion, chopped finely

100 g (3½ oz) smoked or unsmoked turkey rashers, chopped finely

300 g (10½ oz) plain flour

1 teaspoon salt

1 teaspoon paprika

4 teaspoons baking powder

75 g (2¾ oz) low-fat spread

150 g (5½ oz) reduced-fat mature Cheddar cheese, grated

1 egg

200 ml (7 fl oz) skimmed milk

1 Preheat the oven to Gas Mark 5/ 190°C/375°F. Spray a 12-hole muffin tin with low-fat cooking spray.

2 Spray a medium frying-pan with low-fat cooking spray and heat for a

TOMATO AND HERB LOAF

POINTS

per recipe: $11\frac{1}{2}$ per slice: 1

Ⓥ *if using a free-range egg*

Serves 12

Preparation time: 20 minutes

Cooking time: 50 minutes

Calories per slice: 80

Freezing: recommended

Gold Member Louise Iles from Weston-super-Mare has lost 5 stone following *pure points*™ and recipes like this one help to keep her on track. She likes to invent new recipes and test them out on her friends yet she says that her husband is her best critic as he is so honest! Serve with a Point-free salad.

---

1 small onion, chopped finely

1 medium carrot, grated finely or coarsely

50 g ($1\frac{3}{4}$ oz) button mushrooms, sliced

225 g (8 oz) tomatoes, skinned, de-seeded and chopped

$1\frac{1}{2}$ teaspoons dried mixed herbs

225 g (8 oz) wholemeal self-raising flour

1 teaspoon baking powder

1 egg, beaten

3–4 tablespoons skimmed milk

1 teaspoon Marmite (optional)

salt and freshly ground black pepper

---

1 Preheat the oven to Gas Mark 4/ 180°C/350°F. Line a 1 kg (2 lb 4 oz) loaf tin with baking parchment.

2 Put the onion, carrot, mushrooms, tomatoes and herbs into a large mixing bowl and stir together.

3 Sift the flour, baking powder and seasoning together, then add to the vegetable mixture and stir thoroughly. Stir together the beaten egg, milk and Marmite, if using. Add to the bowl and stir until blended.

4 Transfer the mixture to the prepared tin and bake in the centre of the oven for 50 minutes, or until a skewer inserted into the centre comes out clean. Bake for a few more minutes, if necessary.

5 Cool in the tin for a few minutes, then turn out and cool on a wire rack.

VARIATION For a quick hot snack, top a slice of this tasty loaf with a few slices of tomato and a tablespoon of grated half-fat cheese. Grill until hot and bubbling. Points per serving will be $1\frac{1}{2}$.

Tomato and Herb Loaf: Each slice is only 1 Point!

GOING FOR GOLD

POINTS

per recipe: 19½   per slice: 1

Ⓥ if using a free-range egg

Serves 16

Preparation time: 15 minutes

Cooking time: 15 minutes

Calories per slice: 75

Freezing: recommended

Member Angela Arborn joined Weight
Watchers with her fiancé with a view
to losing weight before they got
married. This recipe was one that
Angela developed to allow them
both a sweet snack, without the
dreaded guilt complex.

100 g (3½ oz) wholemeal self-raising
flour

---

100 g (3½ oz) white self-raising flour

50 g (1¾ oz) low-fat spread

25 g (1 oz) glacé cherries, chopped

25 g (1 oz) caster sugar

1 egg

450 ml (16 fl oz) skimmed milk

8 glacé cherries, halved

---

1 Preheat the oven to Gas Mark 6/
200°C/400°F.

2 Put the two types of flour in a
mixing bowl and mix them together.
Add the low-fat spread and rub
in, using your fingertips, until the
mixture resembles fine breadcrumbs.

3 Add the chopped cherries and
sugar to the rubbed-in mixture. Beat
the egg and milk together, then add
just enough to the mixture to make
a soft, but not sticky, dough. Knead
lightly on a work surface sprinkled

with a little flour for a few moments,
until smooth.

4 Divide the mixture into four equal
pieces and roll each piece into a
ball. Flatten out with your hand to
a thickness of 1 cm (½-inch). Place
on lightly greased baking trays
and cut a deep cross into each one,
to divide into four. Brush with
remaining egg mixture. Top each
section with a halved glacé cherry.

5 Bake for 10–15 minutes until risen
and golden brown.

VARIATIONS Use 75 g (2¾ oz)
dried ready-to-eat apricots instead of
the glacé cherries. Points per serving
will be the same.

If you like, add a good pinch of
mixed spice or ground cinnamon to
the scone mixture.

NO-FAT BARA BRITH

POINTS

per recipe: 39   per slice: 3

Ⓥ if using a free-range egg

Serves 14

Preparation time: 10 minutes +
overnight standing

Cooking time: 1¼–1½ hours

Calories per slice: 200

Freezing: recommended

Christine Parkman from Barry in
South Glamorgan has developed a
delicious low-fat version of a Welsh
family favourite, Bara Brith, a moist
dark fruit cake. Since becoming
a Member, Christine has improved
her health and fitness and feels
much better for it!

---

250 g (9 oz) dark muscovado sugar

250 g (9 oz) mixed dried fruit

250 ml (9 fl oz) cold tea

low-fat cooking spray

300 g (10½ oz) self-raising flour

1 egg, beaten

---

1 Put the sugar and dried fruit into
a large mixing bowl and cover with
the cold tea. Stir well, then cover and
allow to stand overnight.

2 Next day, preheat the oven to Gas
Mark 4/180°C/350°F. Grease a 1 kg
(2 lb 4 oz) loaf tin with low-fat
cooking spray and line with
greaseproof paper.

3 Gradually add the flour and egg
to the soaked fruit mixture. When
thoroughly mixed, transfer to the
prepared tin and bake for 1¼ hours.
To test that the cake is cooked, insert
a skewer into the centre of the cake
– it should come out clean. If not,
return to the oven for another few
minutes.

4 Cool in the tin on a wire rack,
and when completely cold, turn out,
wrap in foil and keep for 2–3 days
before cutting.

TOP TIP The cake is moist enough
to eat alone but if you wish, spread
it with 1 teaspoon of low-fat spread
adding a further ½ Point per slice.